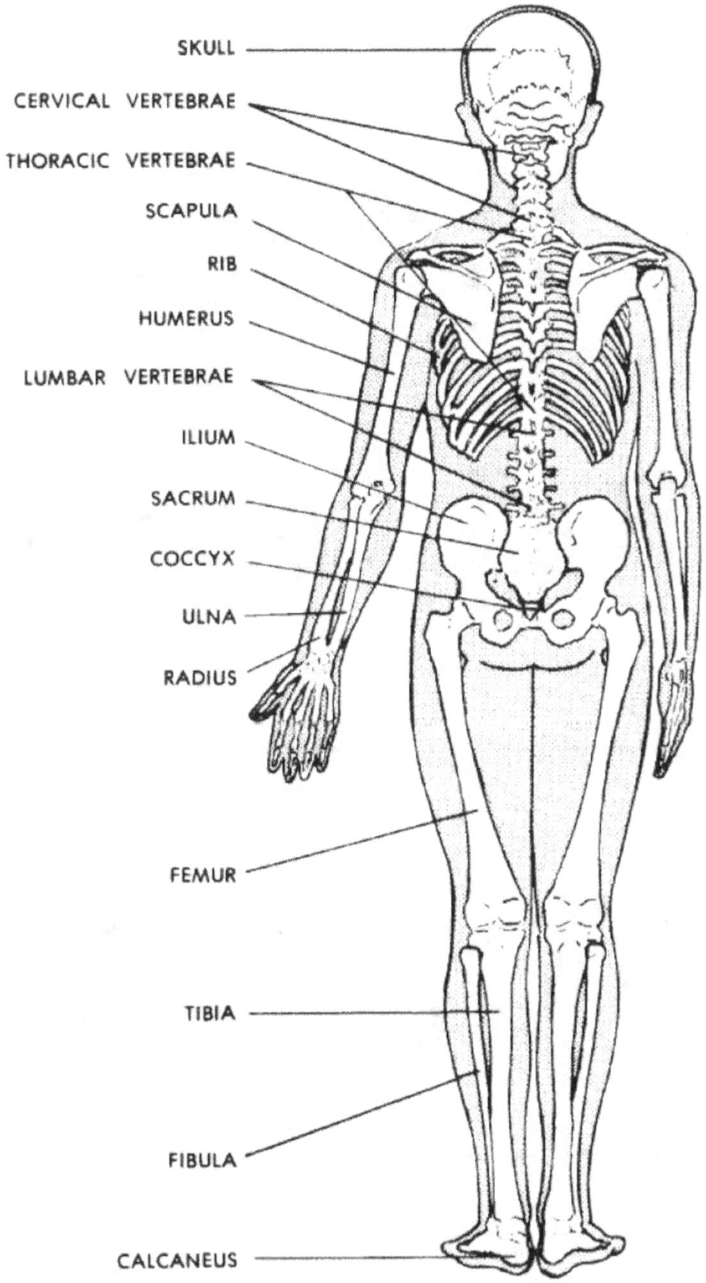
SKULL
CERVICAL VERTEBRAE
THORACIC VERTEBRAE
SCAPULA
RIB
HUMERUS
LUMBAR VERTEBRAE
ILIUM
SACRUM
COCCYX
ULNA
RADIUS
FEMUR
TIBIA
FIBULA
CALCANEUS

This Book Belongs To

____

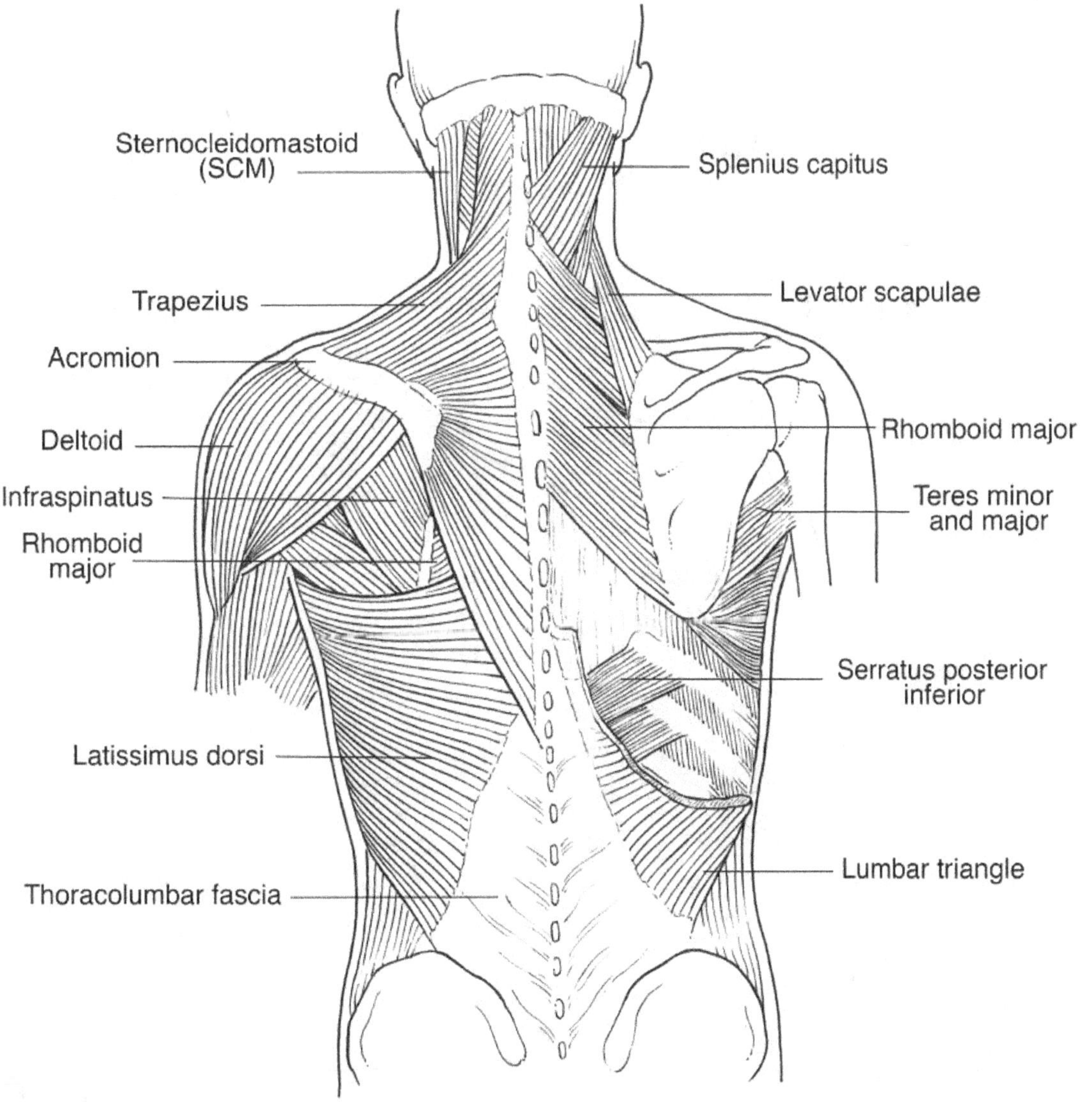

Sternocleidomastoid
(SCM)
Splenius capitus
Trapezius
Levator scapulae
Acromion
Deltoid
Rhomboid major
Infraspinatus
Teres minor
and major
Rhomboid
major
Serratus posterior
inferior
Latissimus dorsi
Thoracolumbar fascia
Lumbar triangle

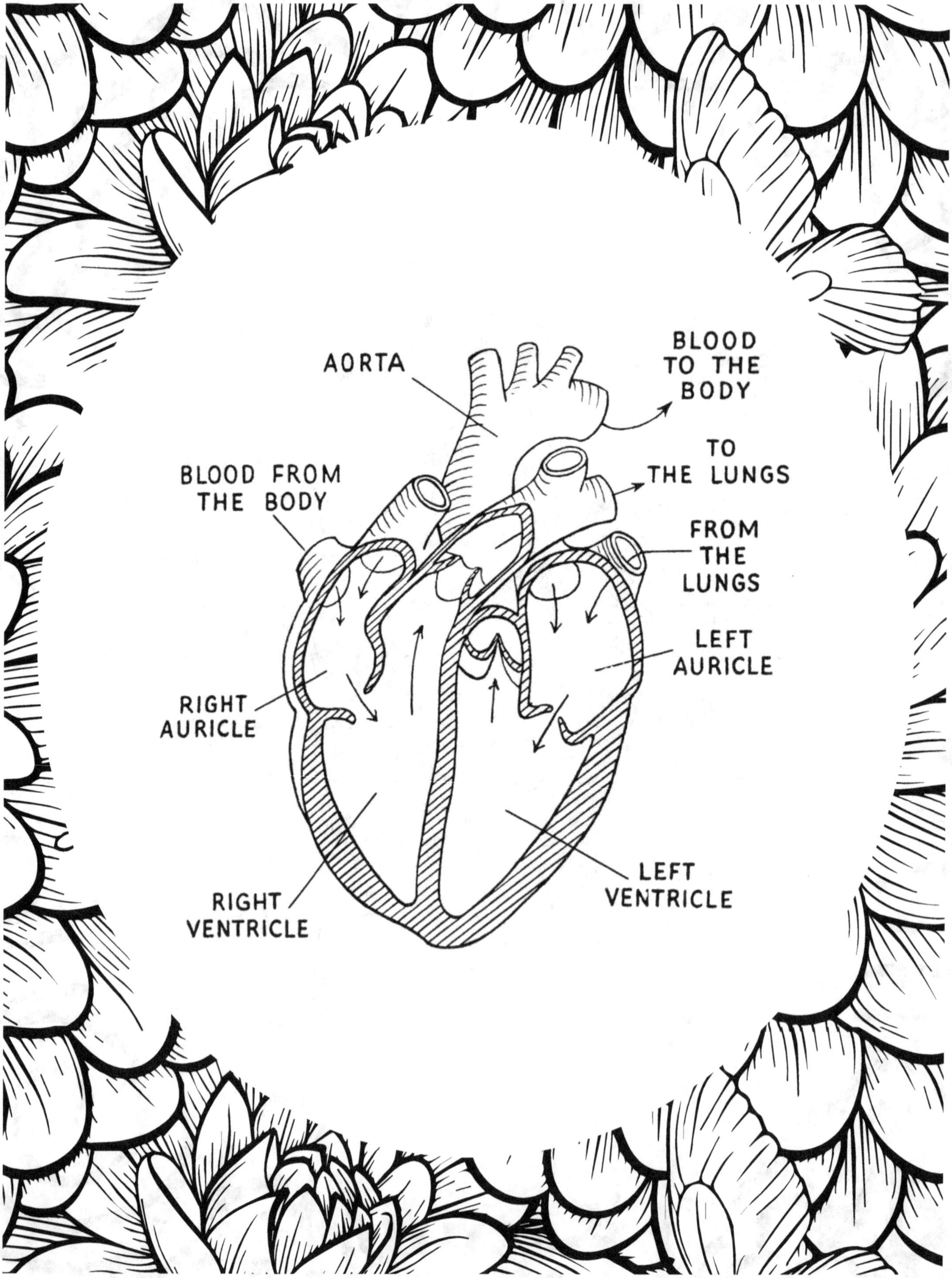
AORTA
BLOOD TO THE BODY
BLOOD FROM THE BODY
TO THE LUNGS
FROM THE LUNGS
LEFT AURICLE
RIGHT AURICLE
LEFT VENTRICLE
RIGHT VENTRICLE

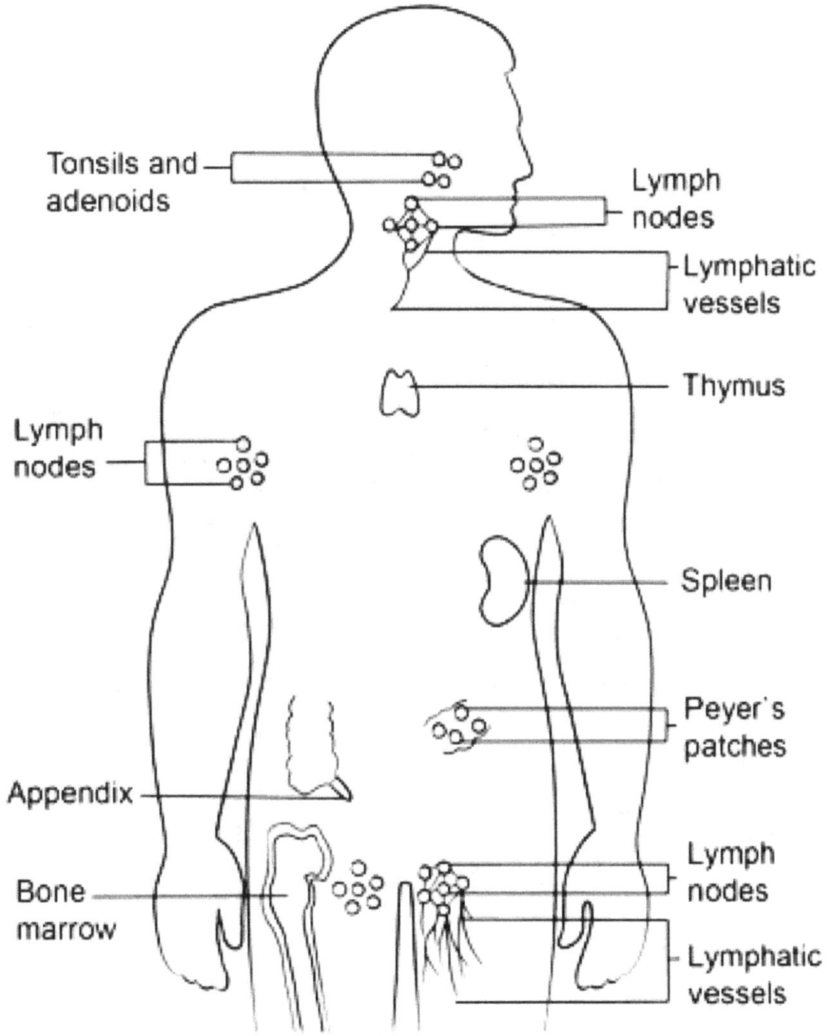

Human Immune System

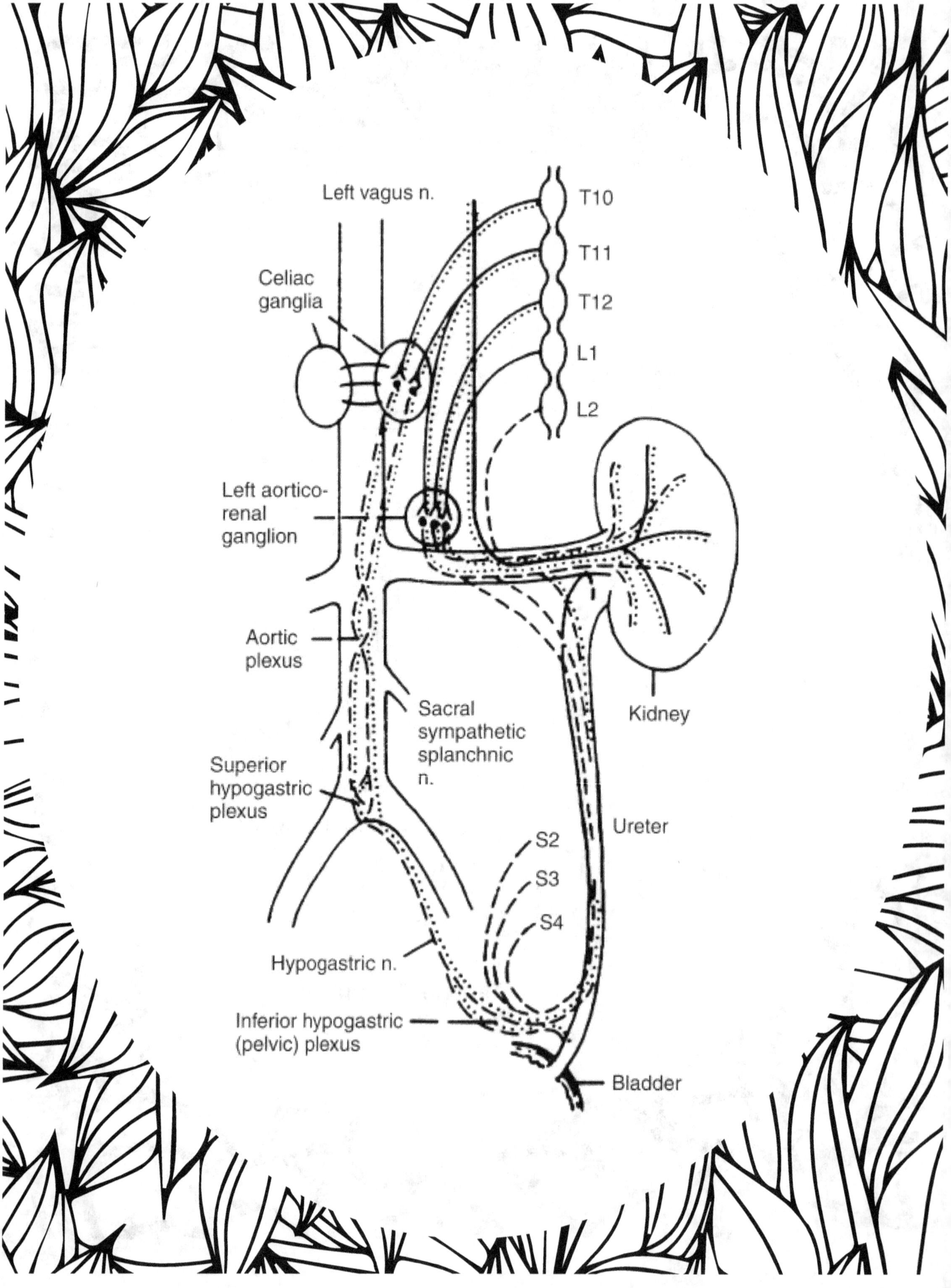
Left vagus n.
T10
T11
T12
L1
L2
Celiac
ganglia
Left aortico-
renal
ganglion
Kidney
Aortic
plexus
Sacral
sympathetic
splanchnic
n.
Superior
hypogastric
plexus
Ureter
S2
S3
S4
Hypogastric n.
Inferior hypogastric
(pelvic) plexus
Bladder

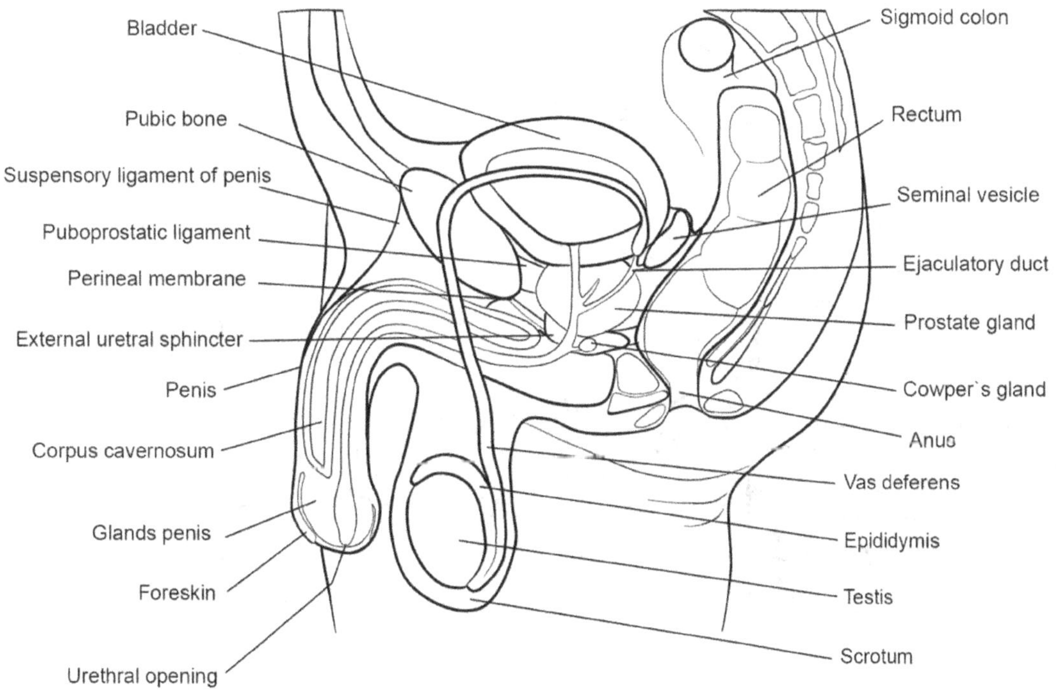

Male reproductive system

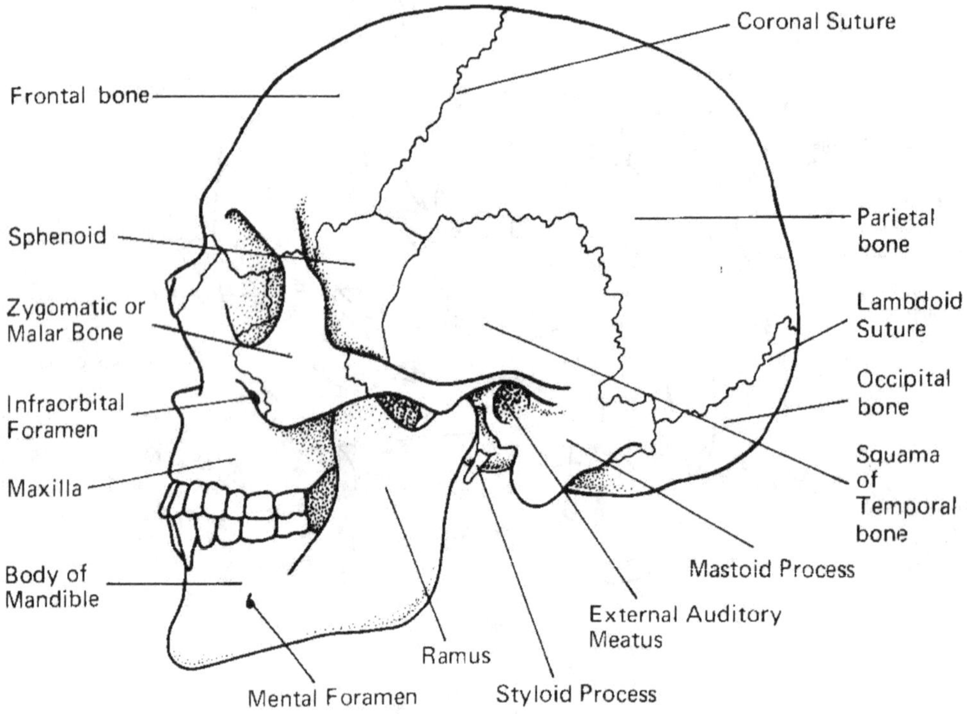

The skull—lateral view.

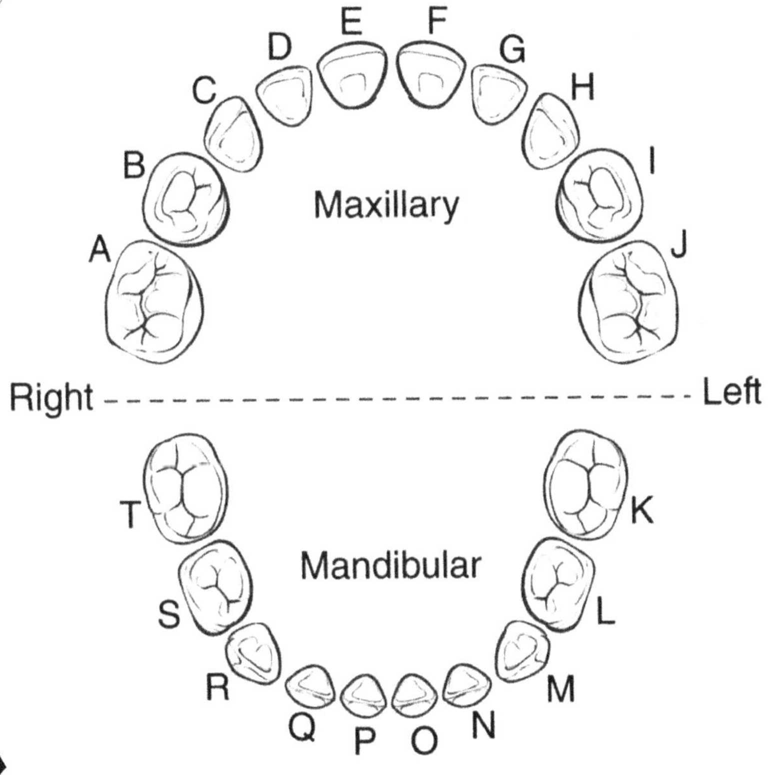

Upper teeth
F. Central incisor
G. Lateral incisor
H. Canine (cuspid)
I. First molar
J. Second molar

Lower teeth
K. Second molar
L. First molar
M. Canine (cuspid)
N. Lateral incisor
O. Central incisor

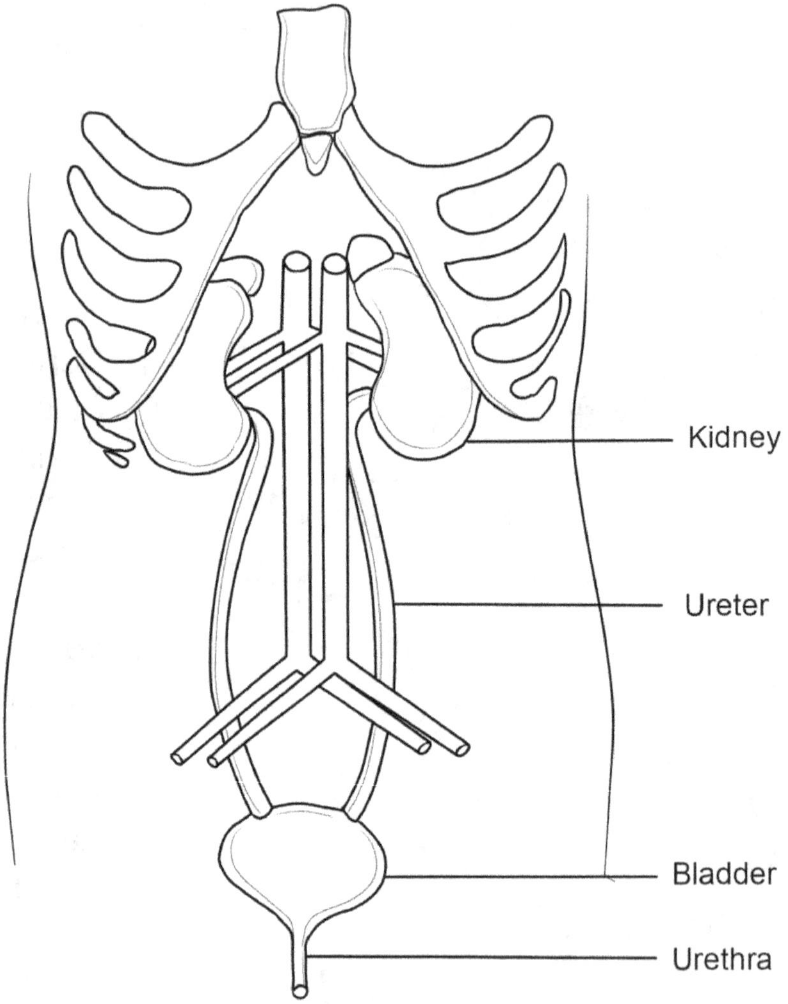

The Urinary System

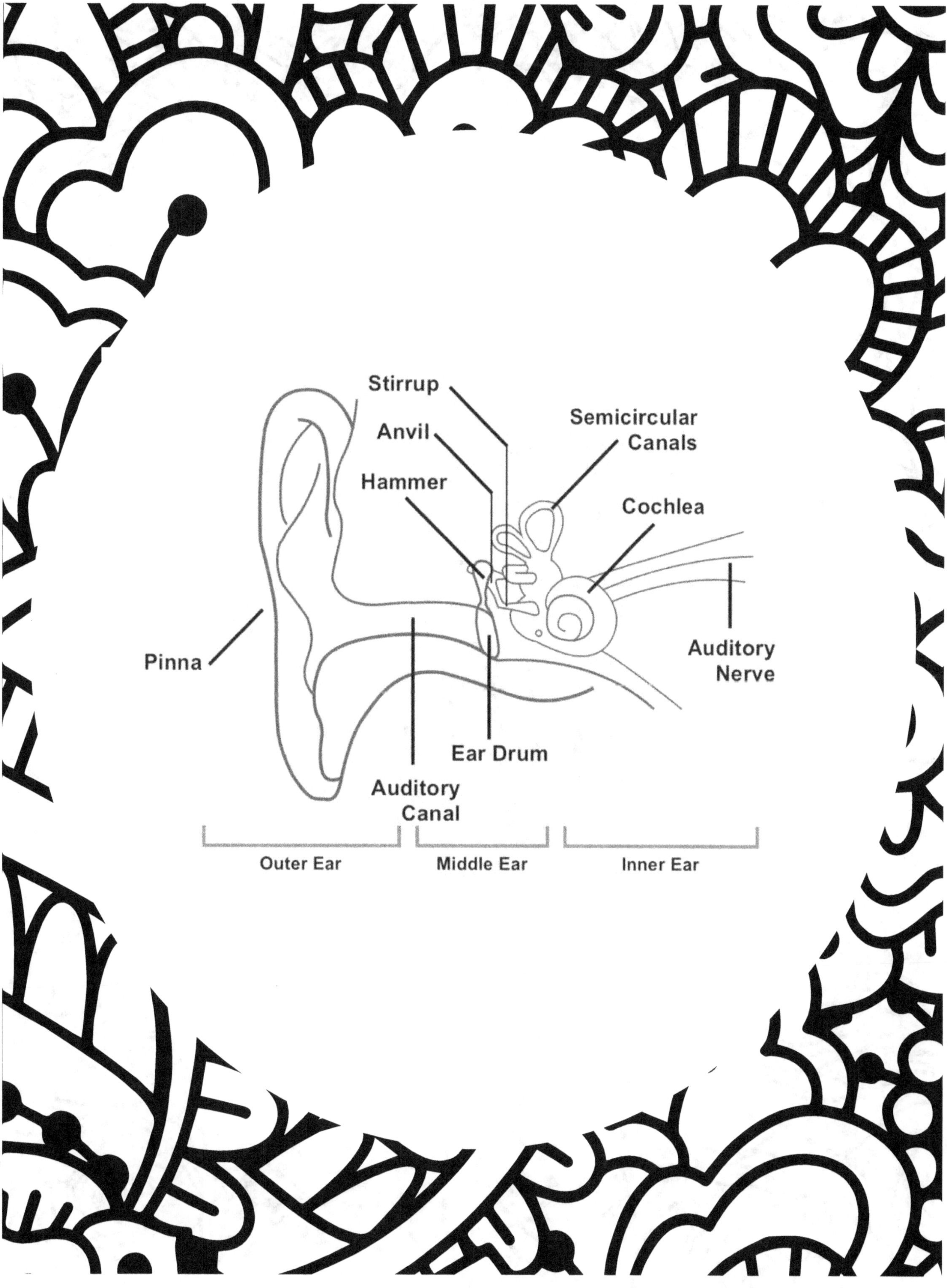
Stirrup
Semicircular Canals
Anvil
Hammer
Cochlea
Pinna
Auditory Nerve
Ear Drum
Auditory Canal
Outer Ear
Middle Ear
Inner Ear

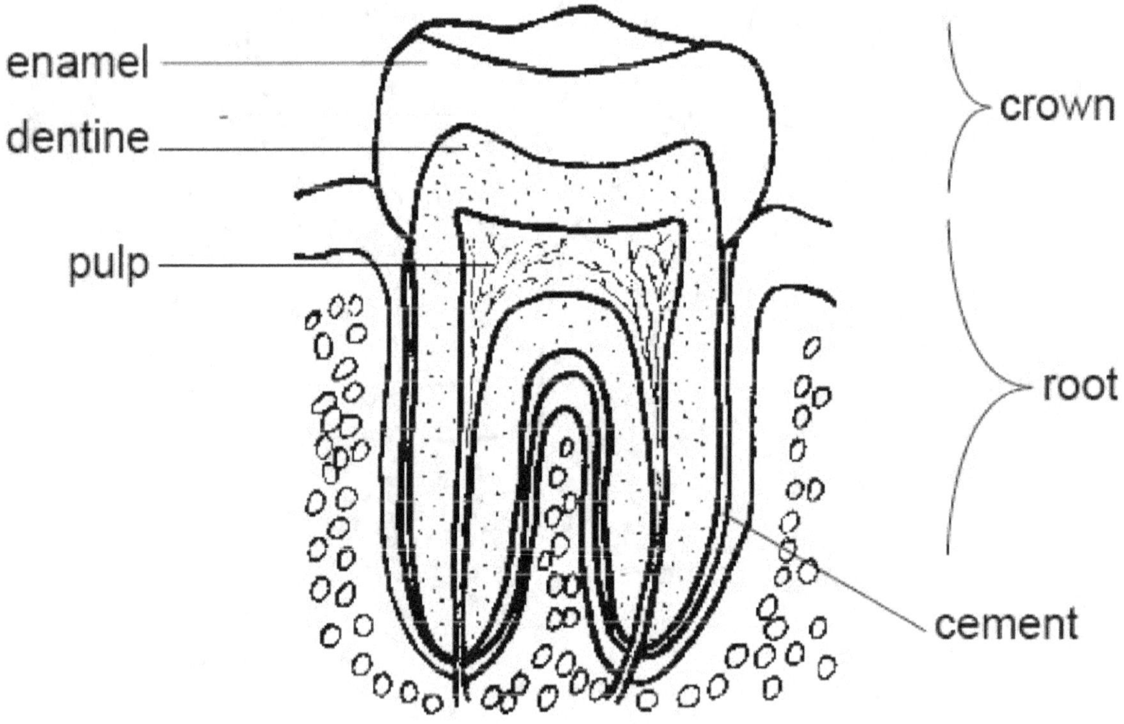
enamel
dentine
pulp
crown
root
cement

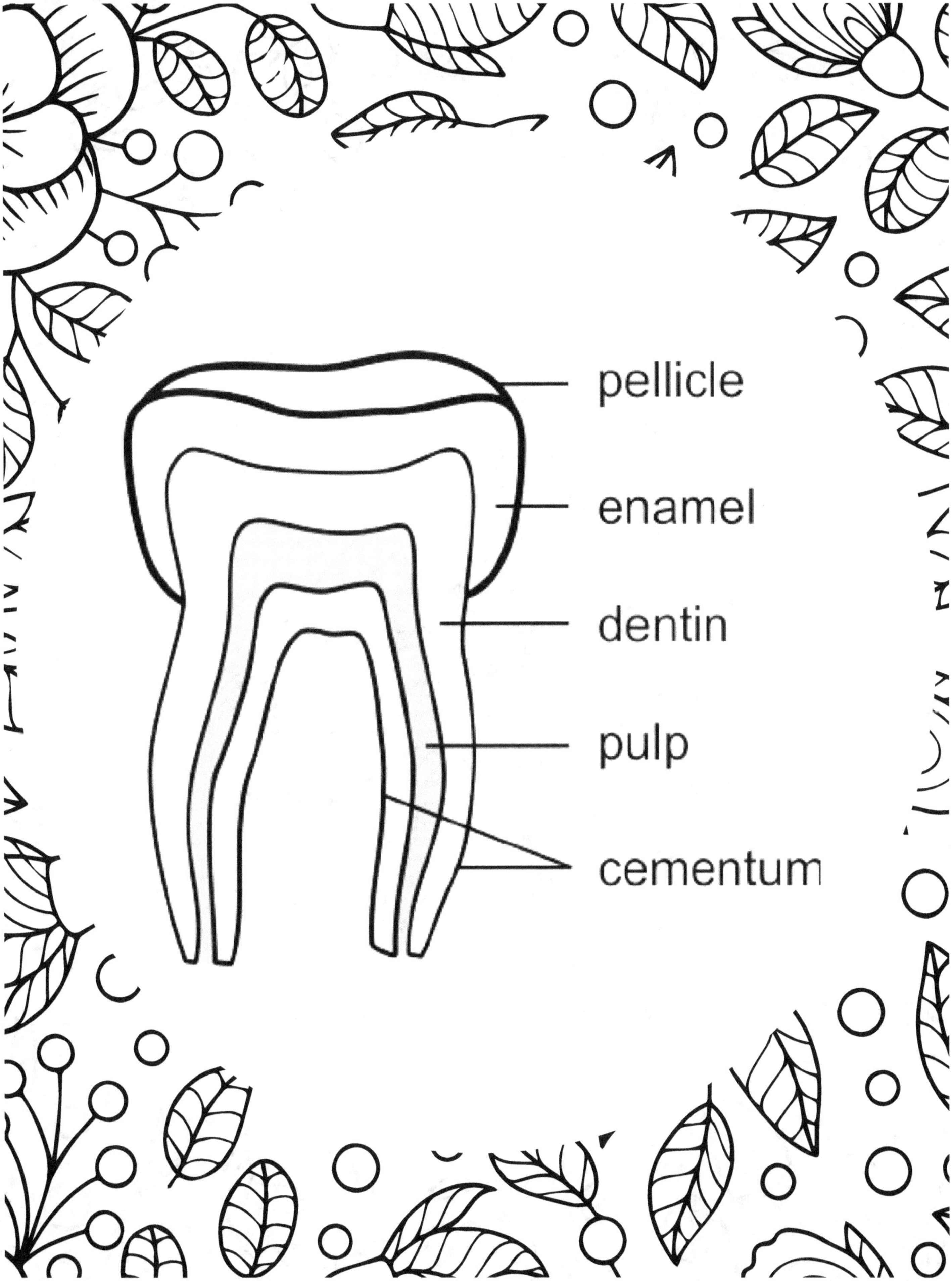
pellicle
enamel
dentin
pulp
cementum

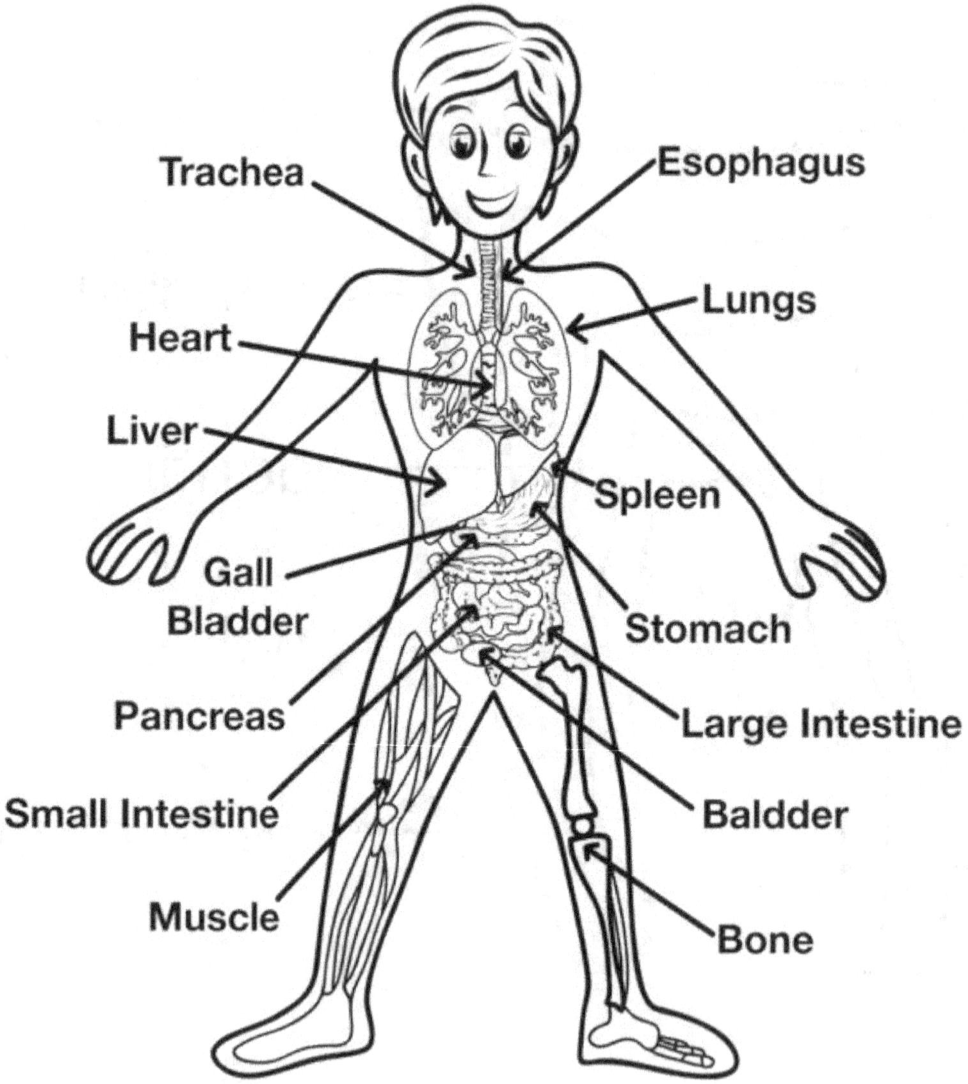
Trachea
Esophagus
Lungs
Heart
Liver
Spleen
Gall Bladder
Stomach
Pancreas
Large Intestine
Small Intestine
Baldder
Muscle
Bone

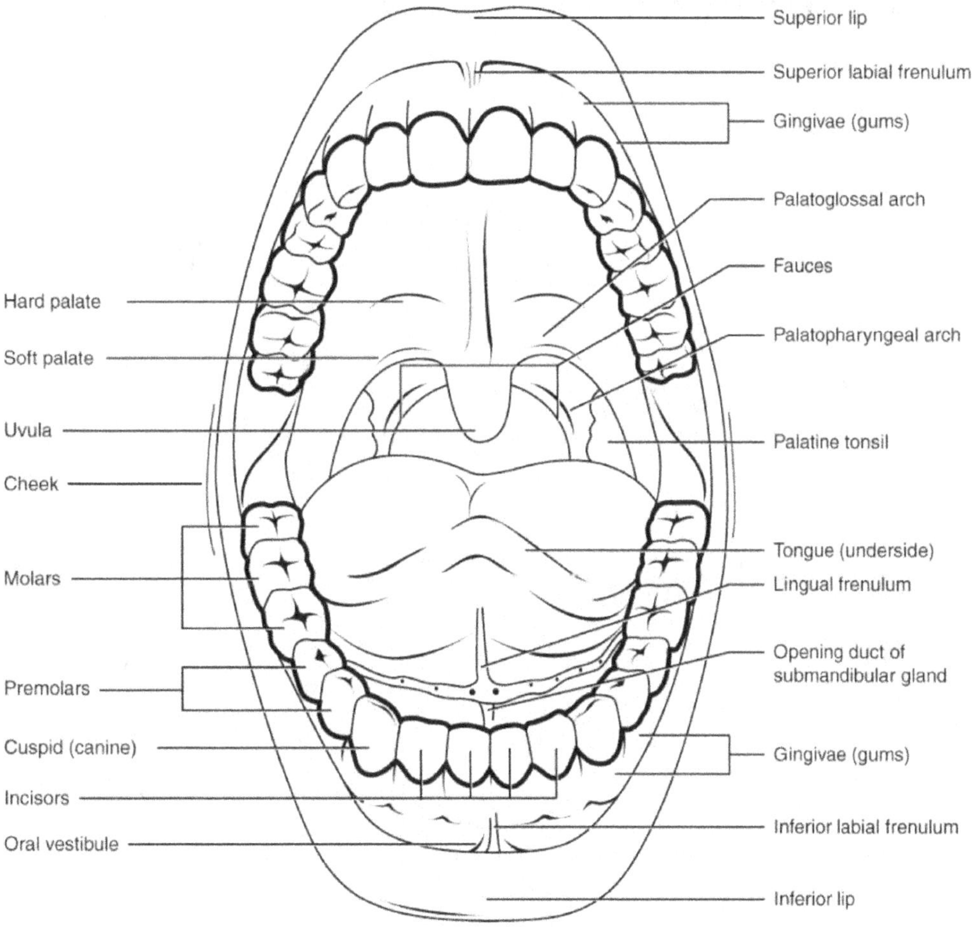

Anterior view

Female Reproductive Organs

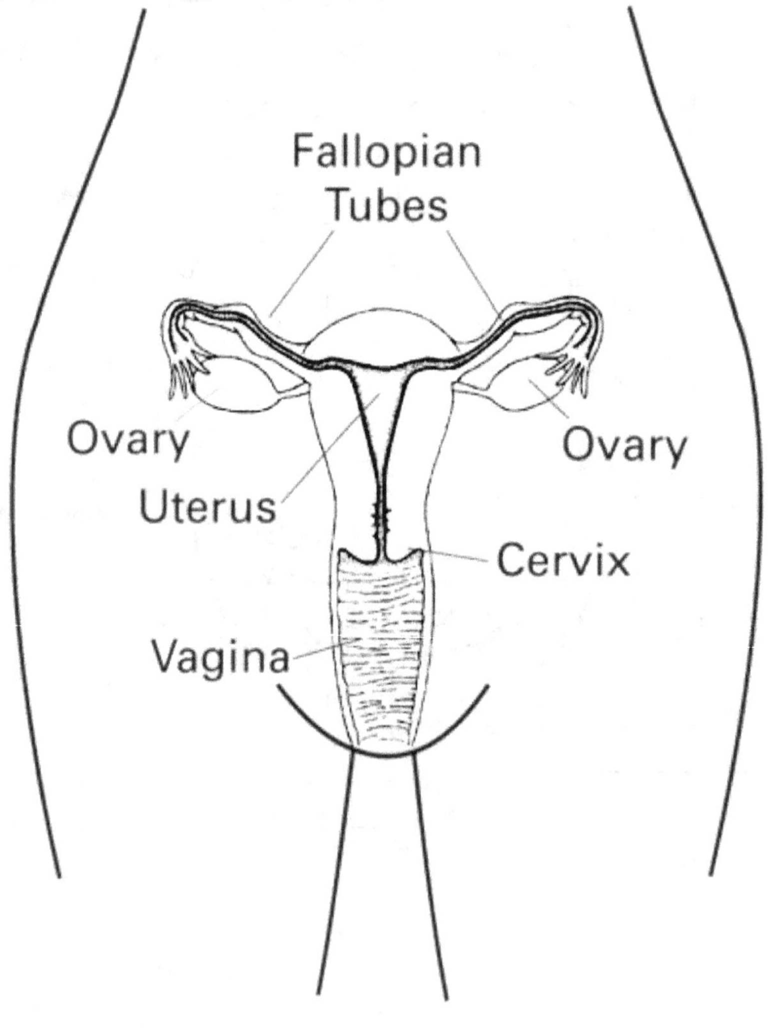

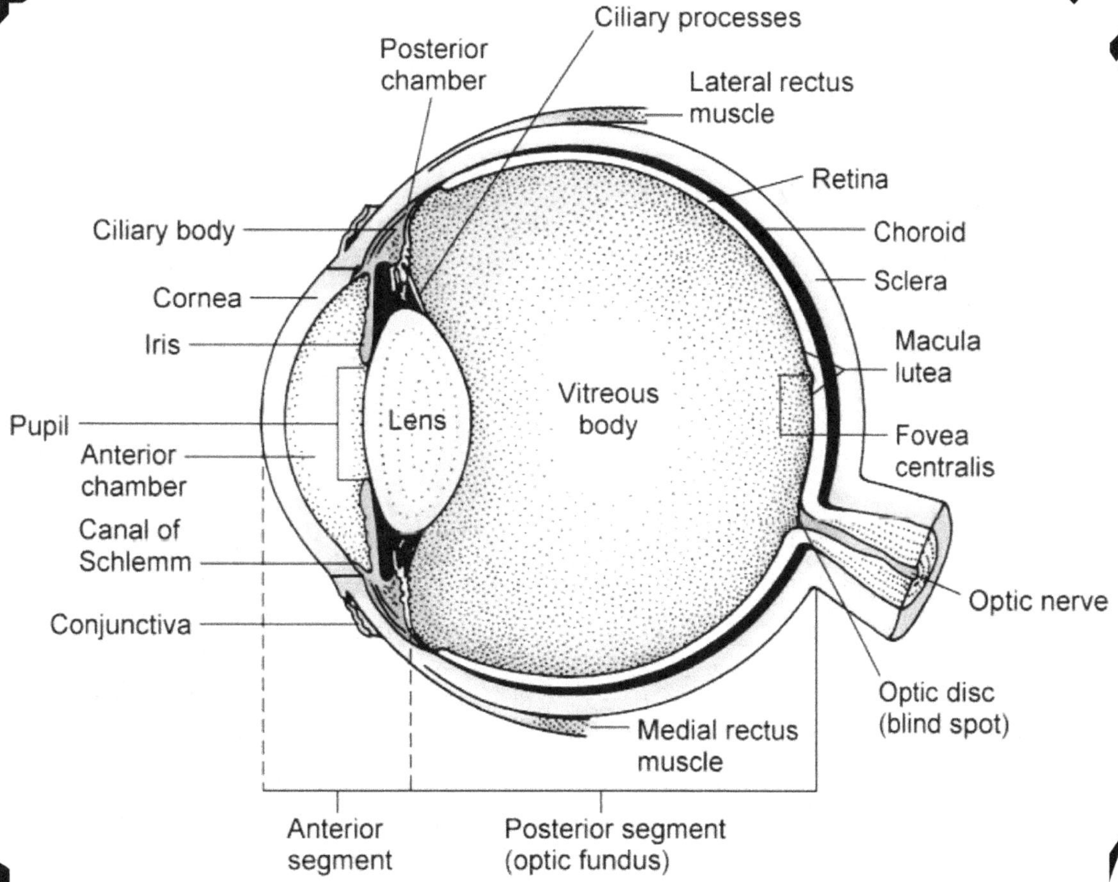
Ciliary processes
Posterior chamber
Lateral rectus muscle
Retina
Ciliary body
Choroid
Cornea
Sclera
Iris
Macula lutea
Vitreous body
Pupil
Lens
Anterior chamber
Fovea centralis
Canal of Schlemm
Optic nerve
Conjunctiva
Optic disc (blind spot)
Medial rectus muscle
Anterior segment
Posterior segment (optic fundus)

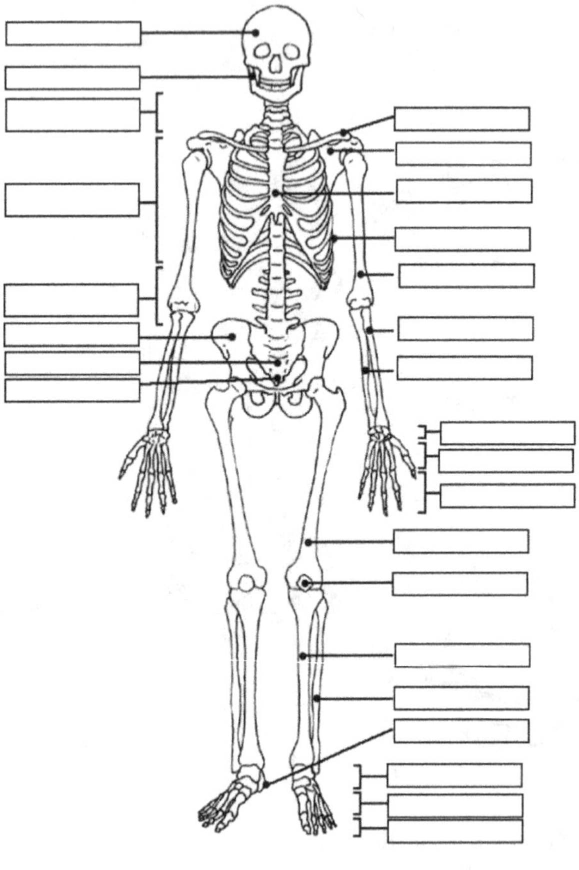

Question

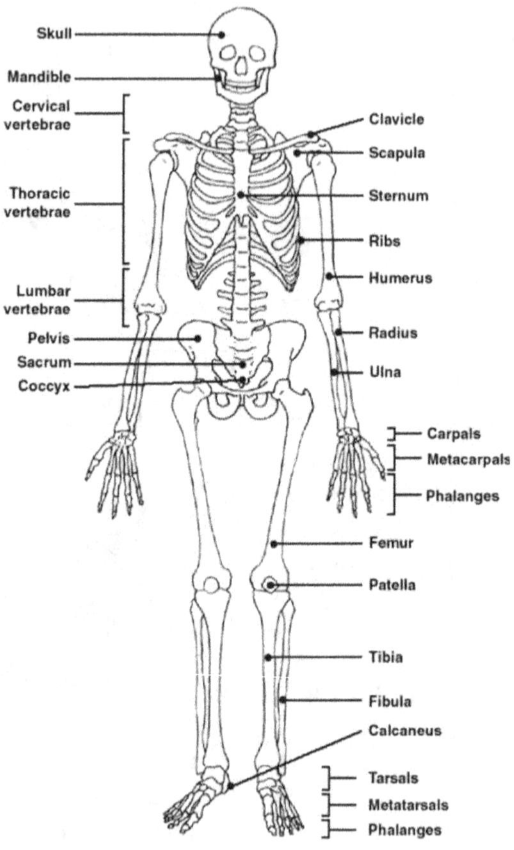

Answer

Anatomy of the Human Eye

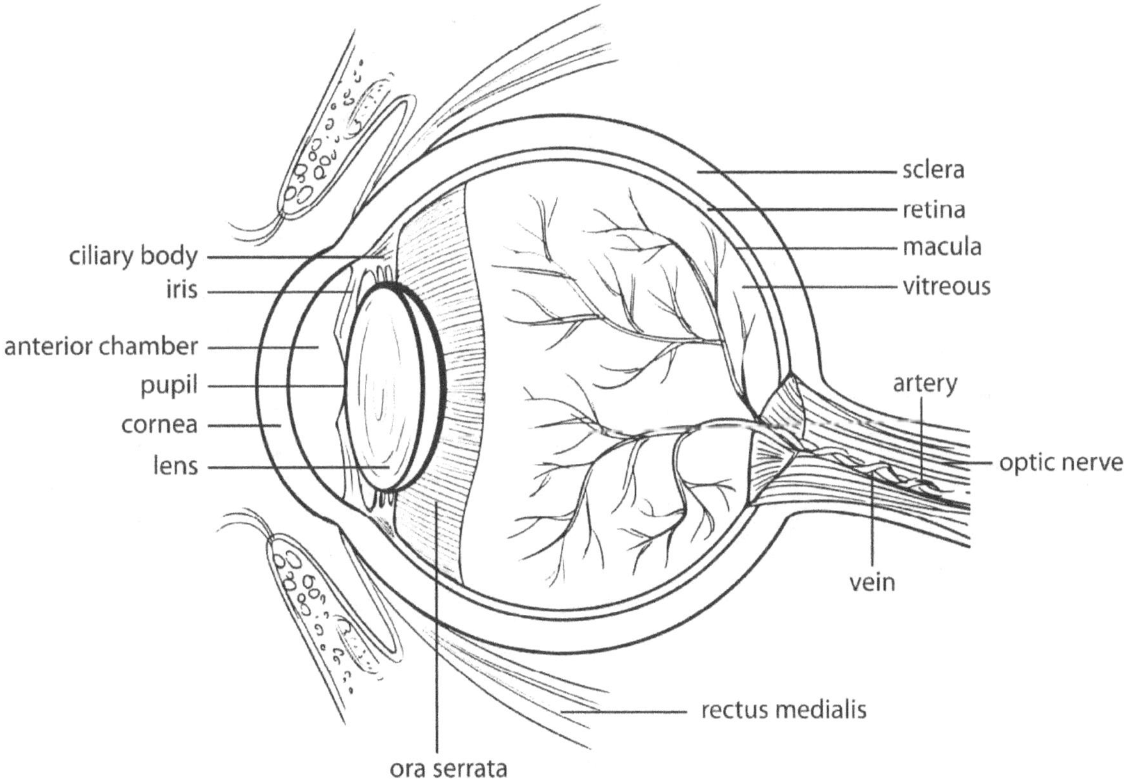

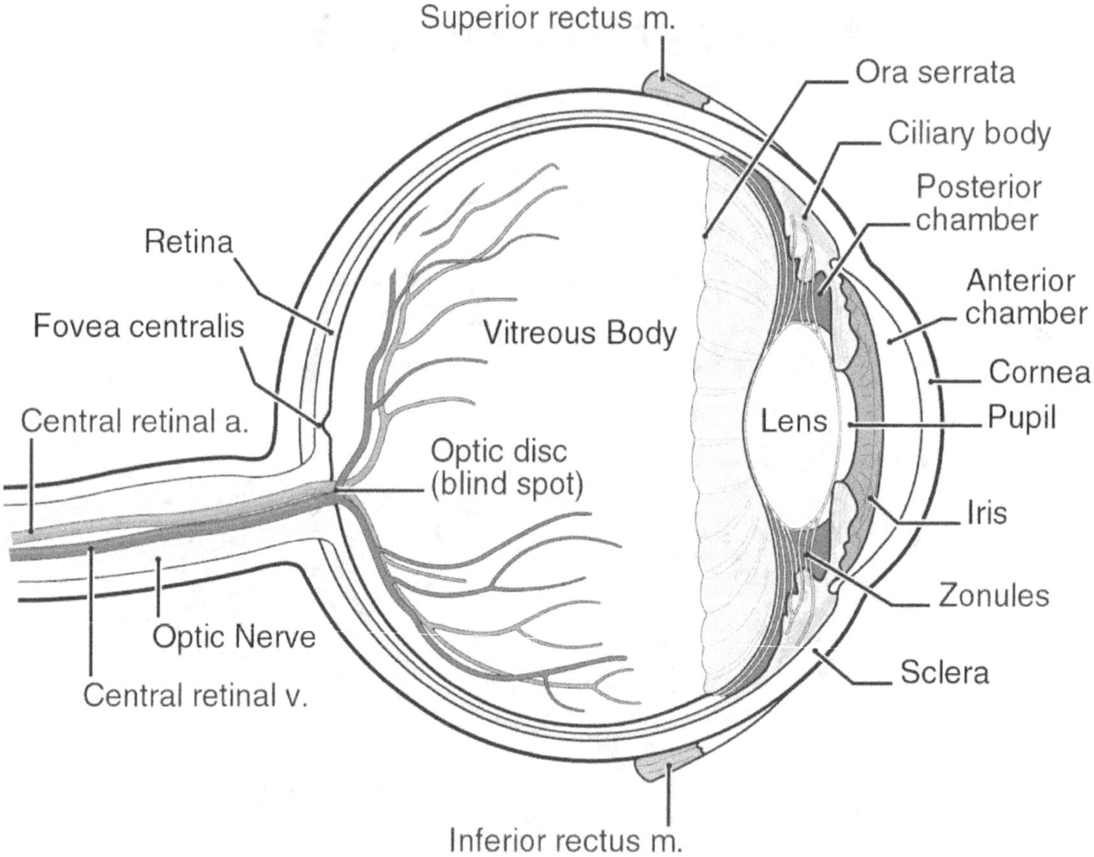
Superior rectus m.
Ora serrata
Ciliary body
Posterior chamber
Anterior chamber
Cornea
Pupil
Iris
Zonules
Sclera
Retina
Fovea centralis
Central retinal a.
Vitreous Body
Lens
Optic disc (blind spot)
Optic Nerve
Central retinal v.
Inferior rectus m.

parts of an ear

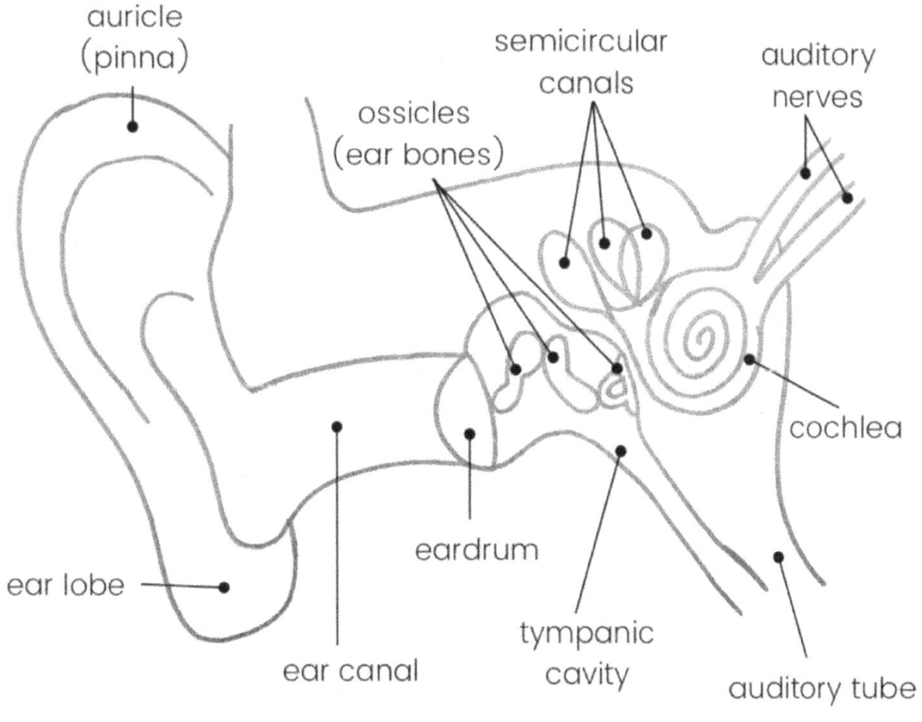

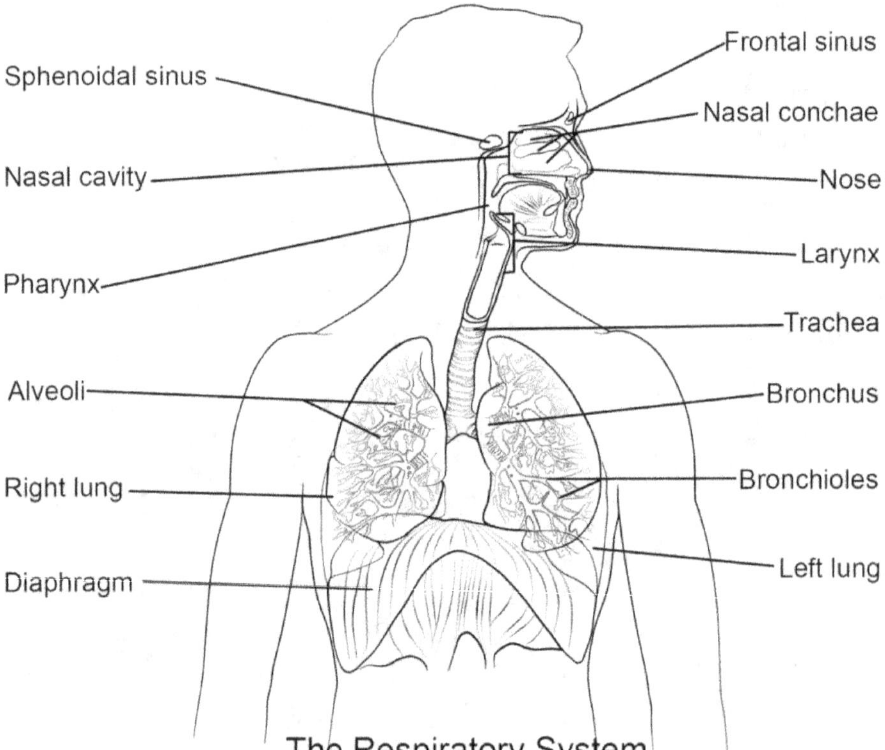

The Respiratory System

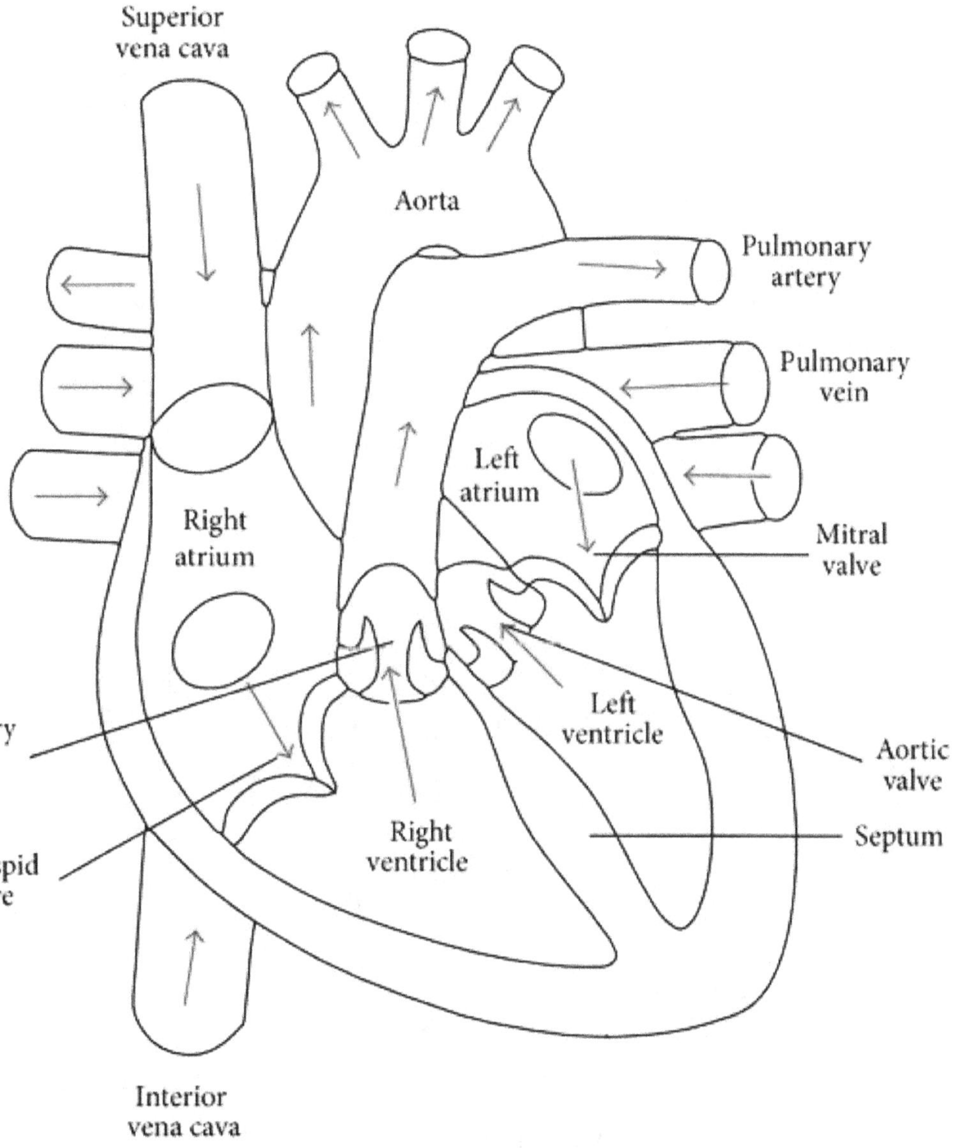
Superior
vena cava
Aorta
Pulmonary
artery
Pulmonary
vein
Left
atrium
Right
atrium
Mitral
valve
Pulmonary
valve
Left
ventricle
Aortic
valve
Septum
Right
ventricle
Tricuspid
valve
Interior
vena cava

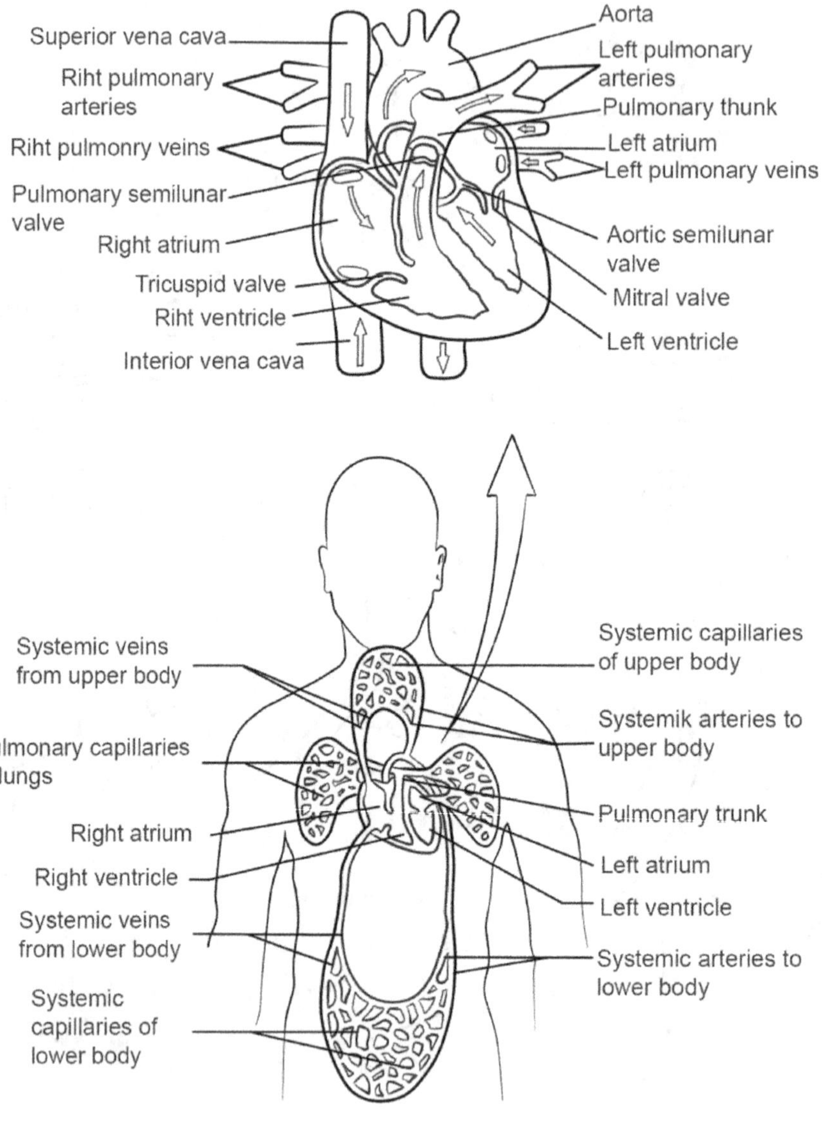

Human Circulatory System

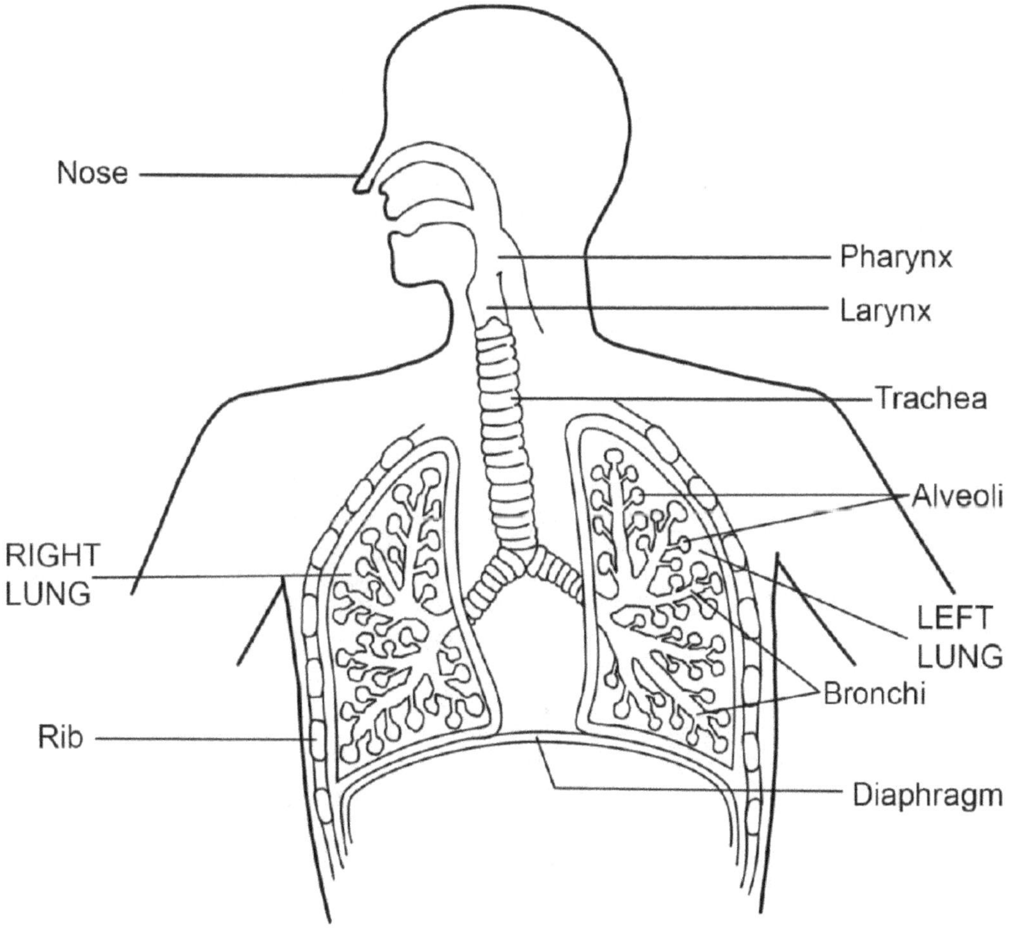
Nose
Pharynx
Larynx
Trachea
Alveoli
RIGHT LUNG
LEFT LUNG
Bronchi
Rib
Diaphragm

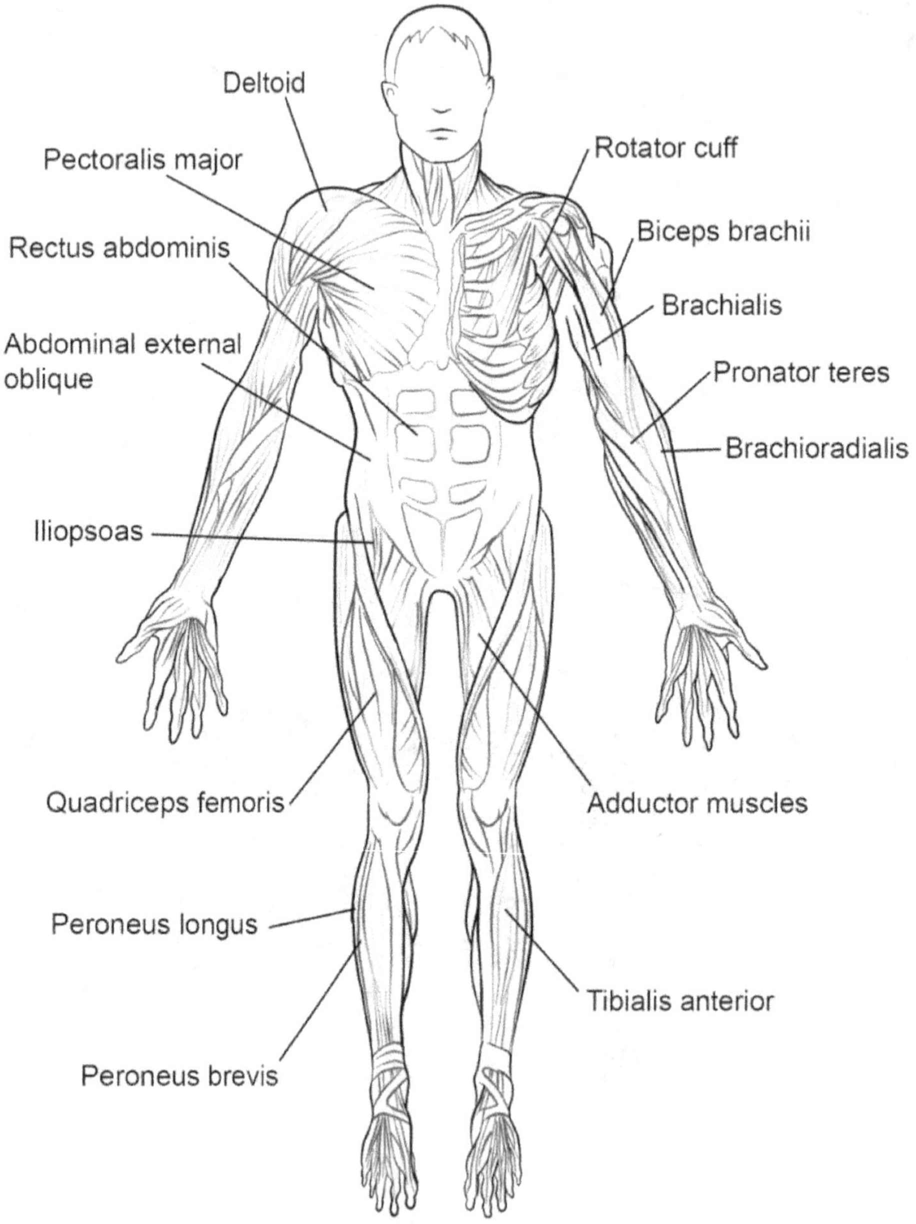

Human Muscles

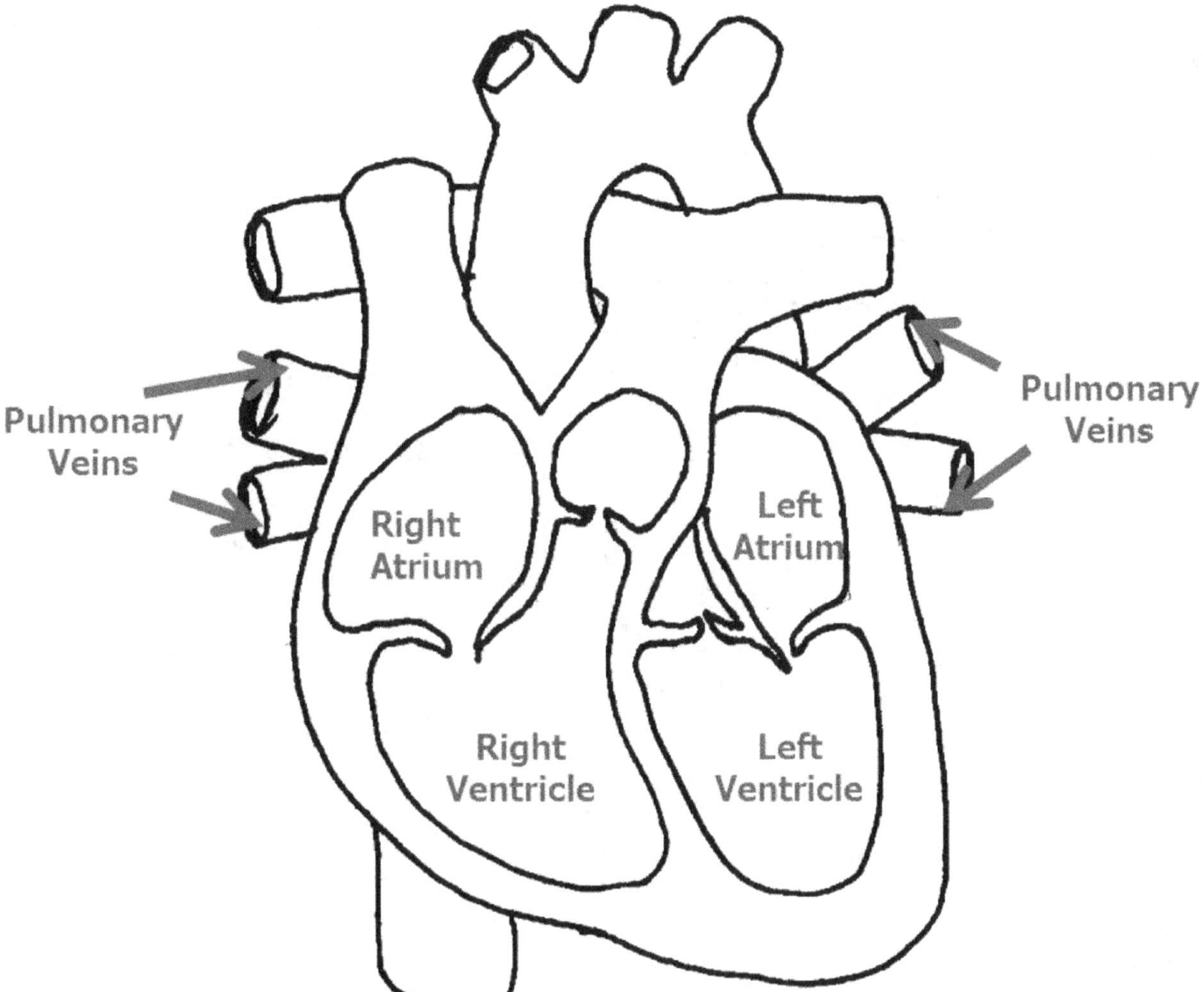

Pulmonary Veins
Right Atrium
Left Atrium
Pulmonary Veins
Right Ventricle
Left Ventricle

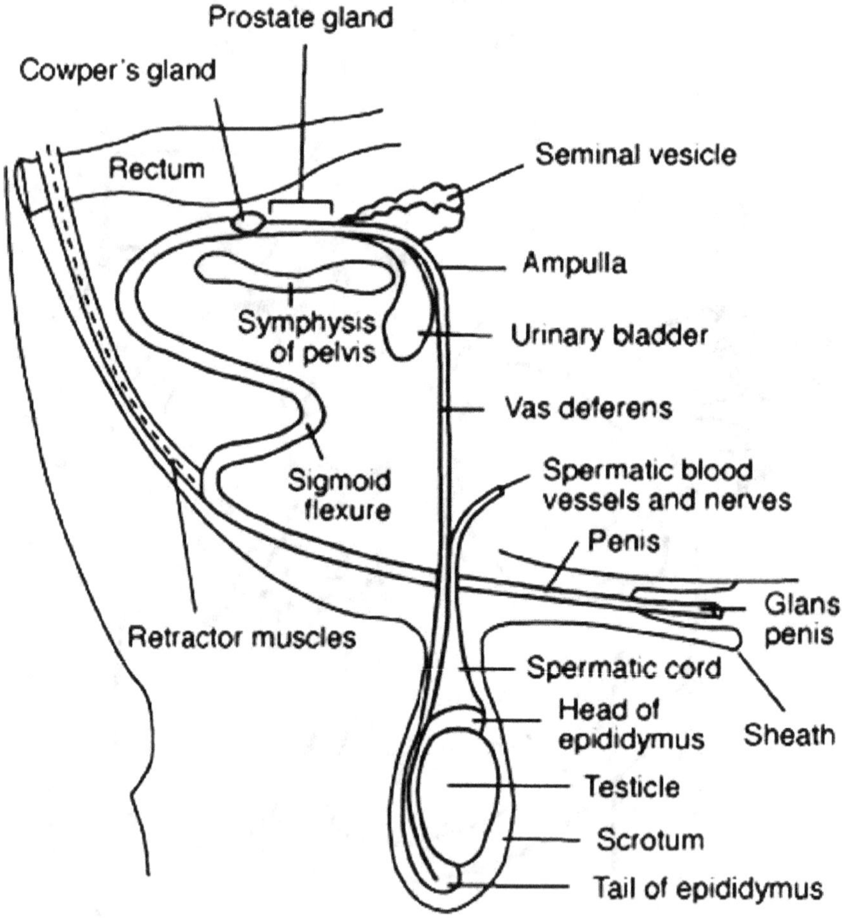
Prostate gland
Cowper's gland
Rectum
Seminal vesicle
Ampulla
Symphysis
of pelvis
Urinary bladder
Vas deferens
Sigmoid
flexure
Spermatic blood
vessels and nerves
Penis
Glans
penis
Retractor muscles
Spermatic cord
Sheath
Head of
epididymus
Testicle
Scrotum
Tail of epididymus

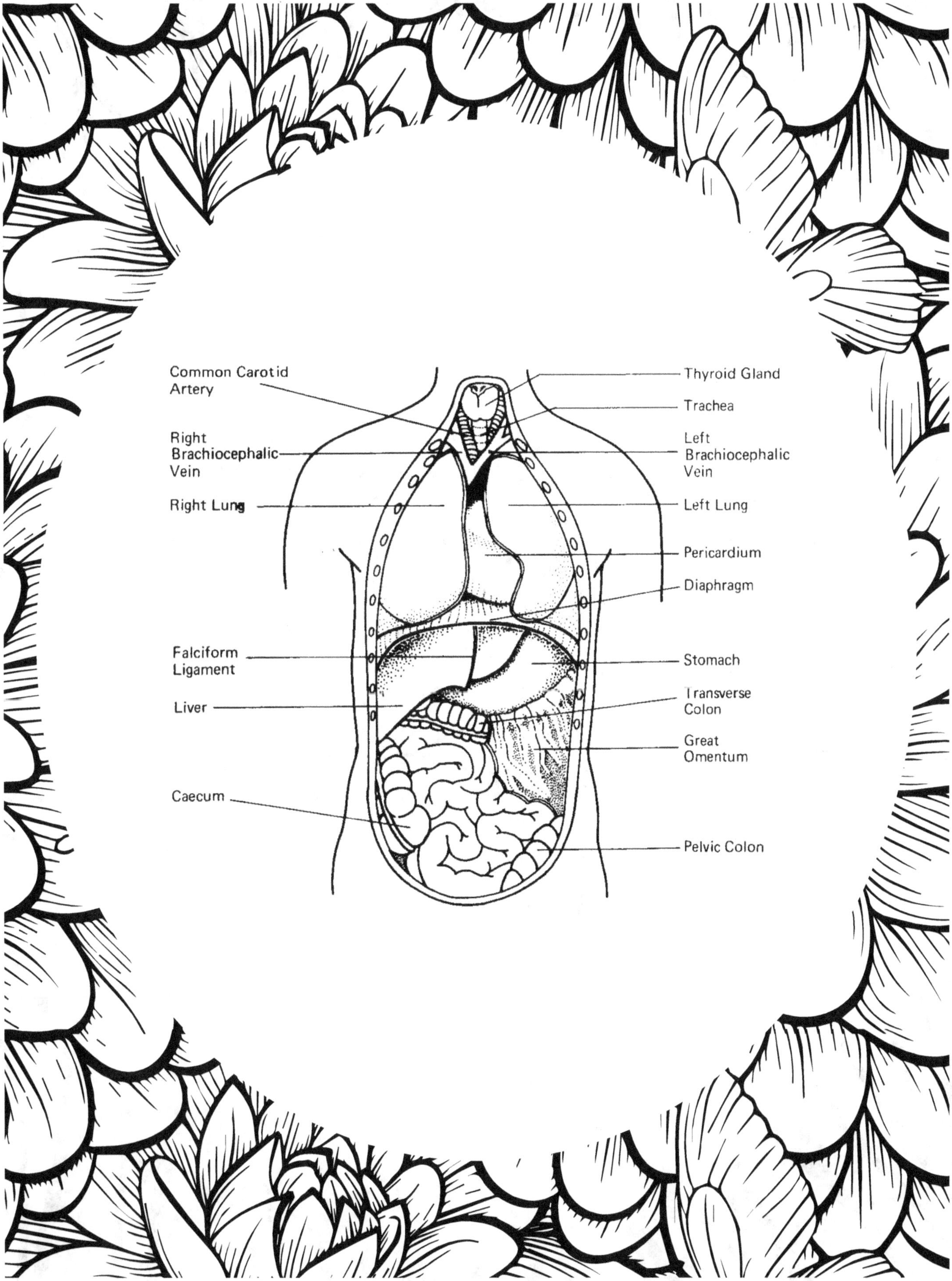
Common Carotid Artery
Right Brachiocephalic Vein
Right Lung
Falciform Ligament
Liver
Caecum
Thyroid Gland
Trachea
Left Brachiocephalic Vein
Left Lung
Pericardium
Diaphragm
Stomach
Transverse Colon
Great Omentum
Pelvic Colon

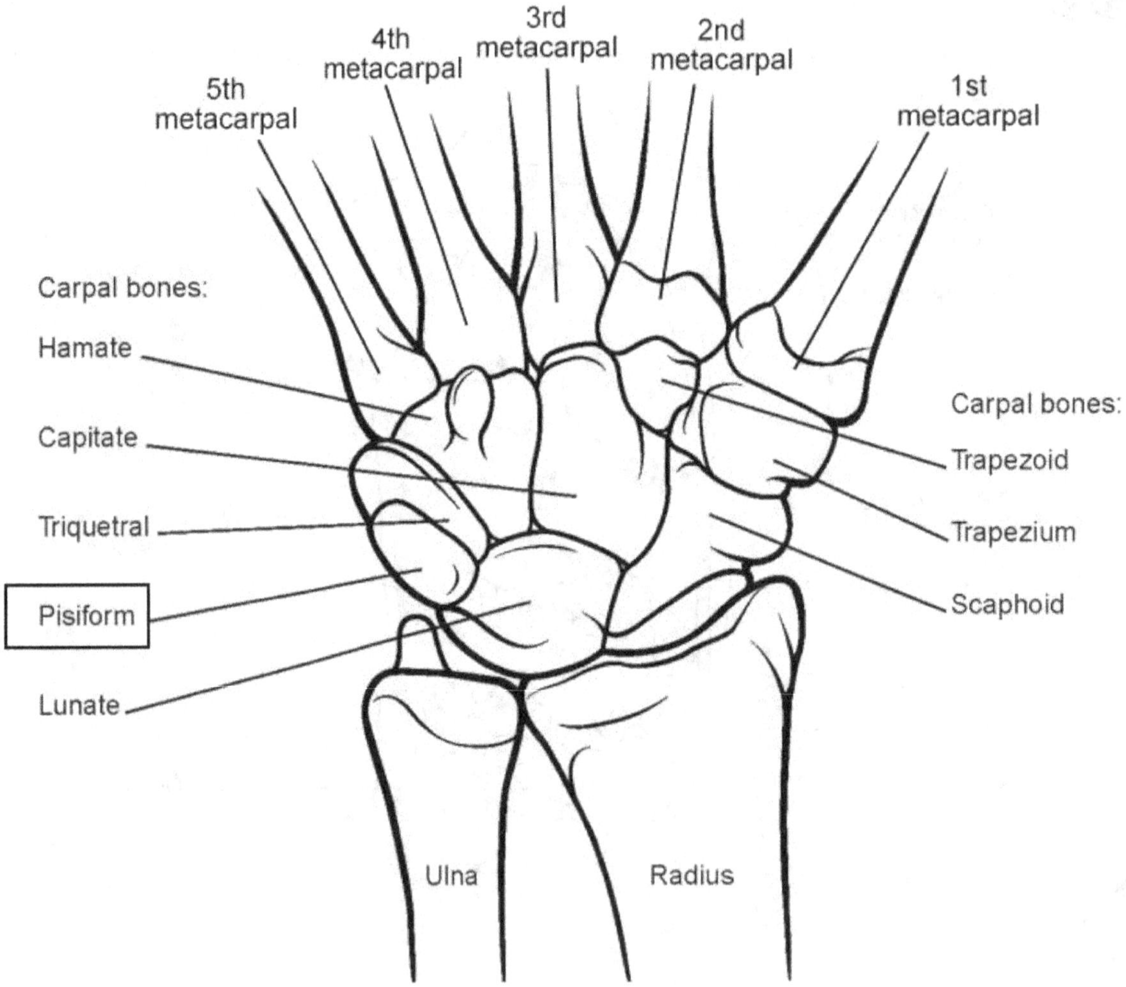
5th metacarpal
4th metacarpal
3rd metacarpal
2nd metacarpal
1st metacarpal
Carpal bones:
Hamate
Capitate
Triquetral
Pisiform
Lunate
Carpal bones:
Trapezoid
Trapezium
Scaphoid
Ulna
Radius

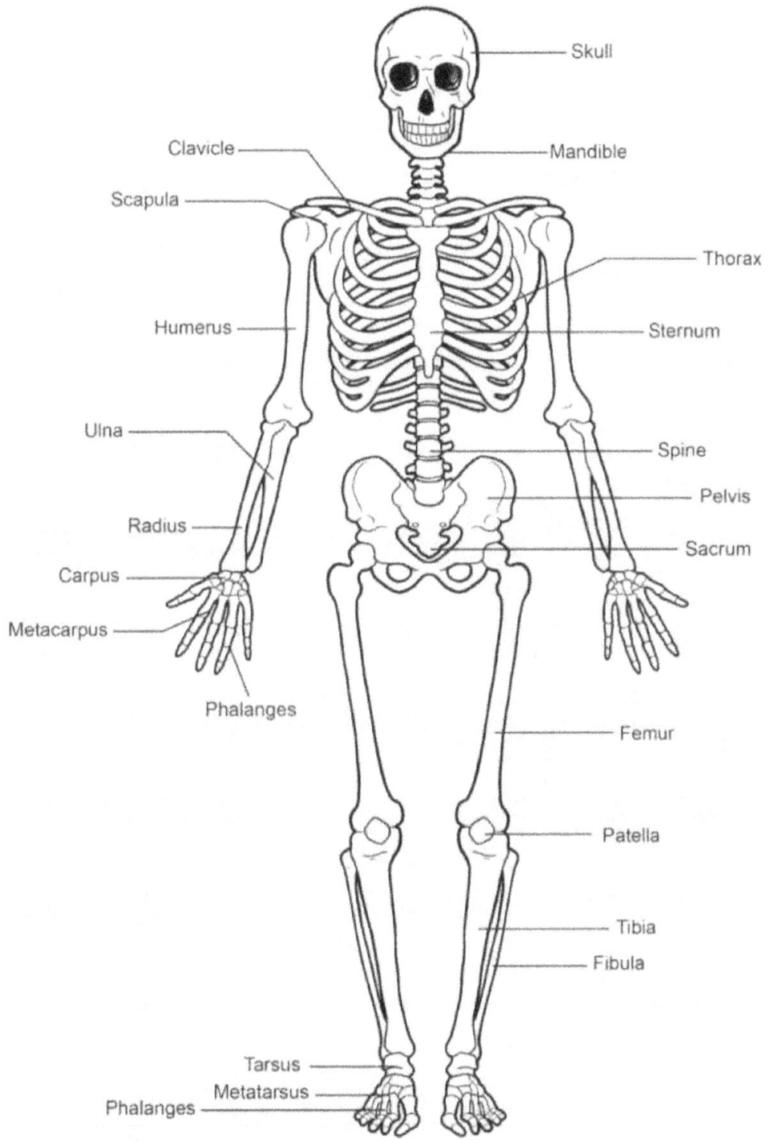
Skull
Clavicle
Mandible
Scapula
Thorax
Humerus
Sternum
Ulna
Spine
Pelvis
Radius
Sacrum
Carpus
Metacarpus
Phalanges
Femur
Patella
Tibia
Fibula
Tarsus
Metatarsus
Phalanges

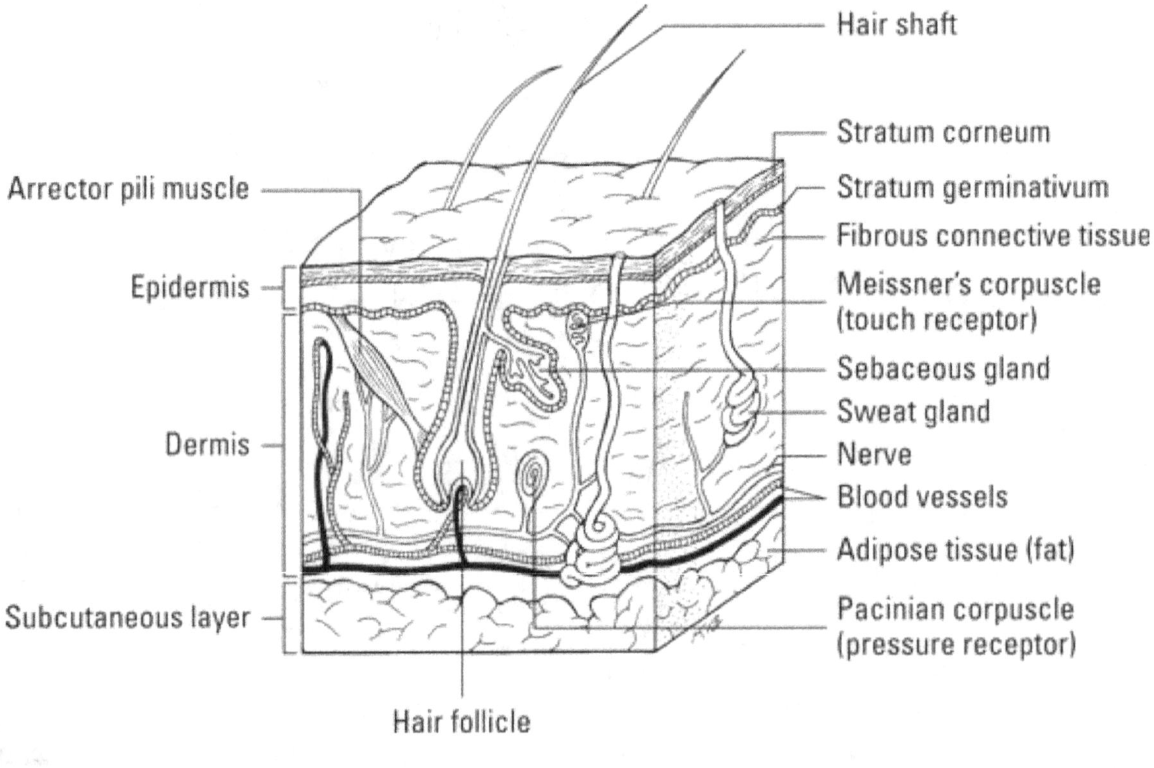
Hair shaft
Stratum corneum
Arrector pili muscle
Stratum germinativum
Fibrous connective tissue
Epidermis
Meissner's corpuscle
(touch receptor)
Sebaceous gland
Sweat gland
Dermis
Nerve
Blood vessels
Adipose tissue (fat)
Subcutaneous layer
Pacinian corpuscle
(pressure receptor)
Hair follicle

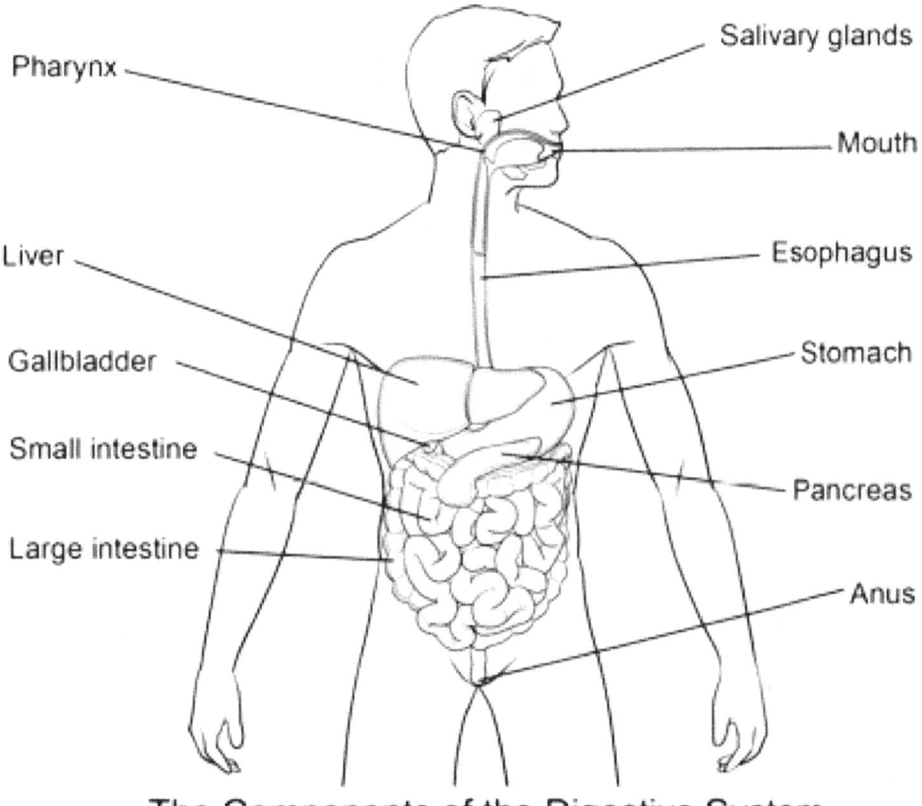

The Components of the Digestive System

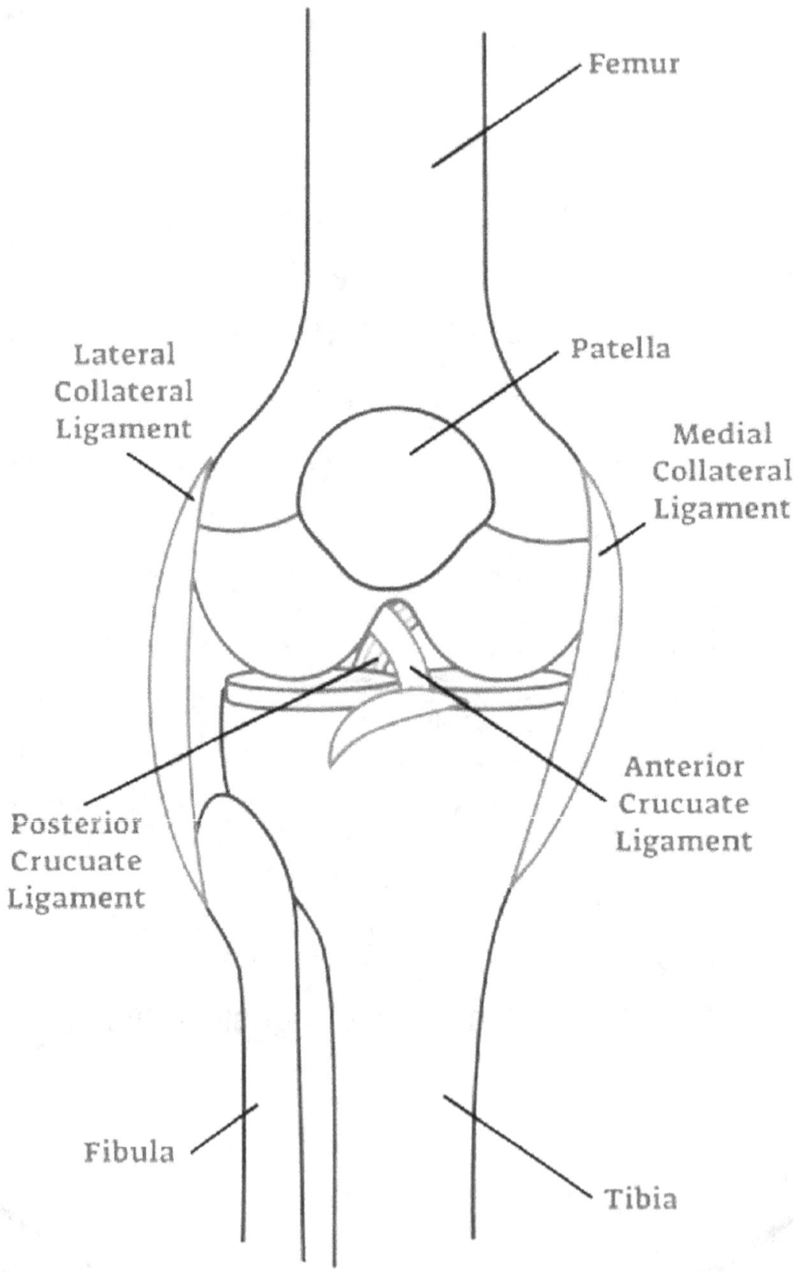
Femur
Lateral Collateral Ligament
Patella
Medial Collateral Ligament
Anterior Crucuate Ligament
Posterior Crucuate Ligament
Fibula
Tibia

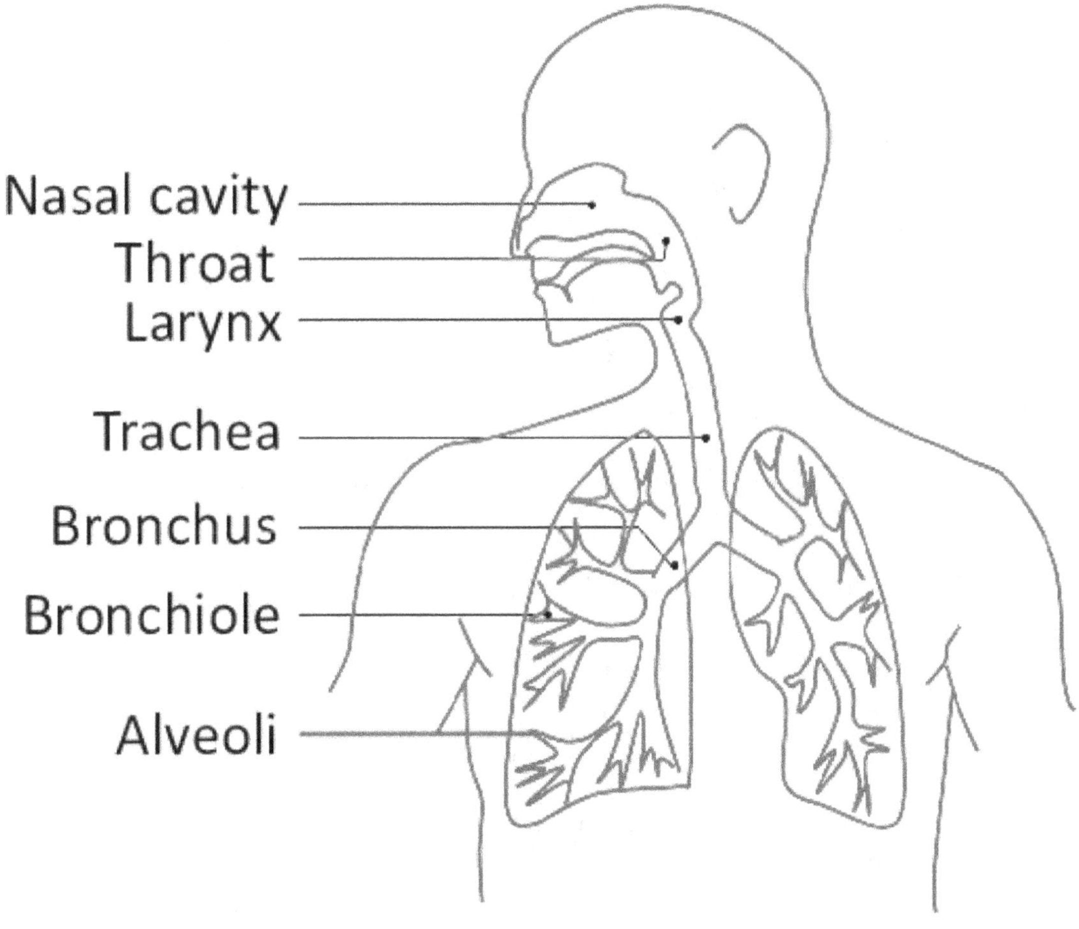
Nasal cavity
Throat
Larynx
Trachea
Bronchus
Bronchiole
Alveoli

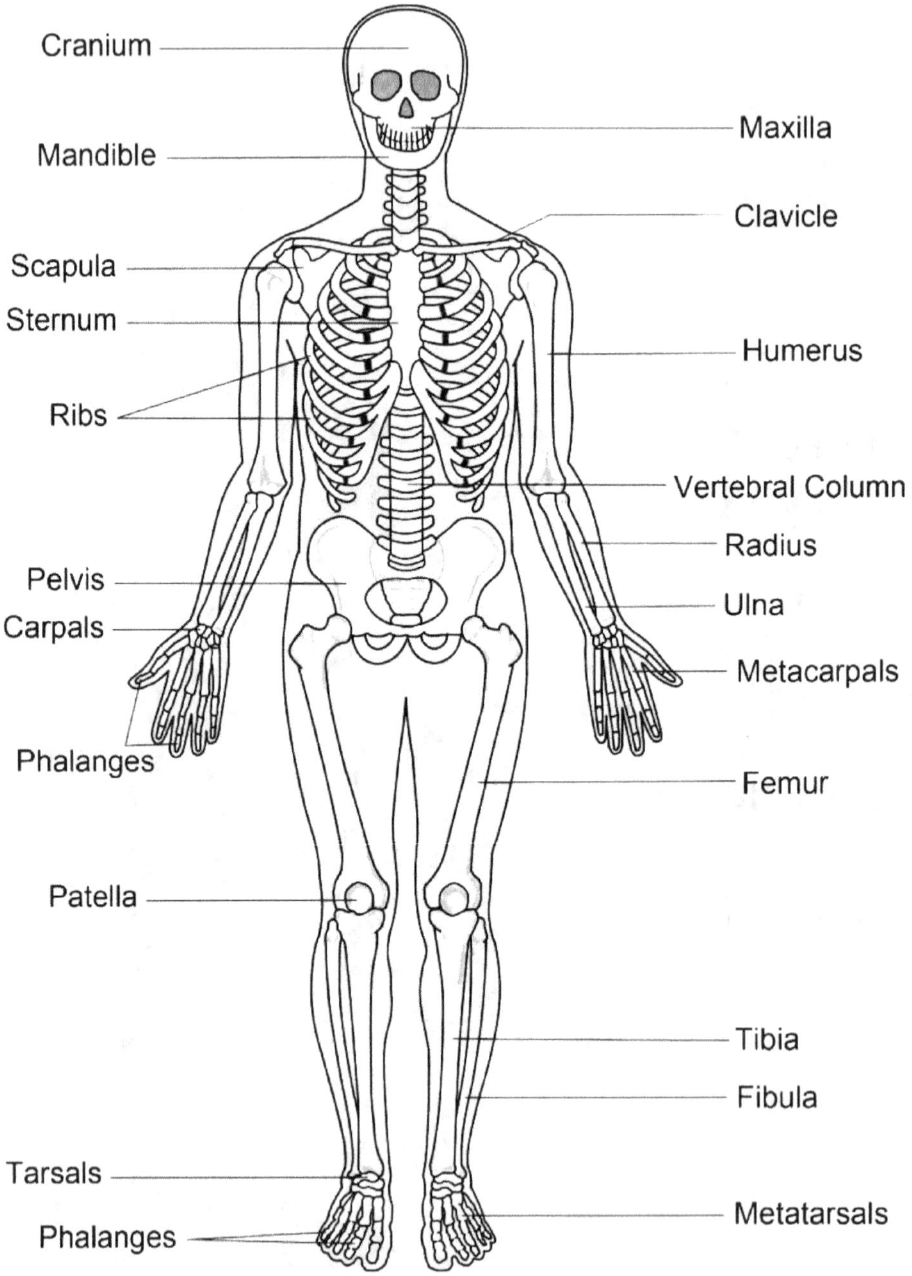
Cranium
Maxilla
Mandible
Clavicle
Scapula
Sternum
Humerus
Ribs
Vertebral Column
Radius
Pelvis
Ulna
Carpals
Metacarpals
Phalanges
Femur
Patella
Tibia
Fibula
Tarsals
Metatarsals
Phalanges

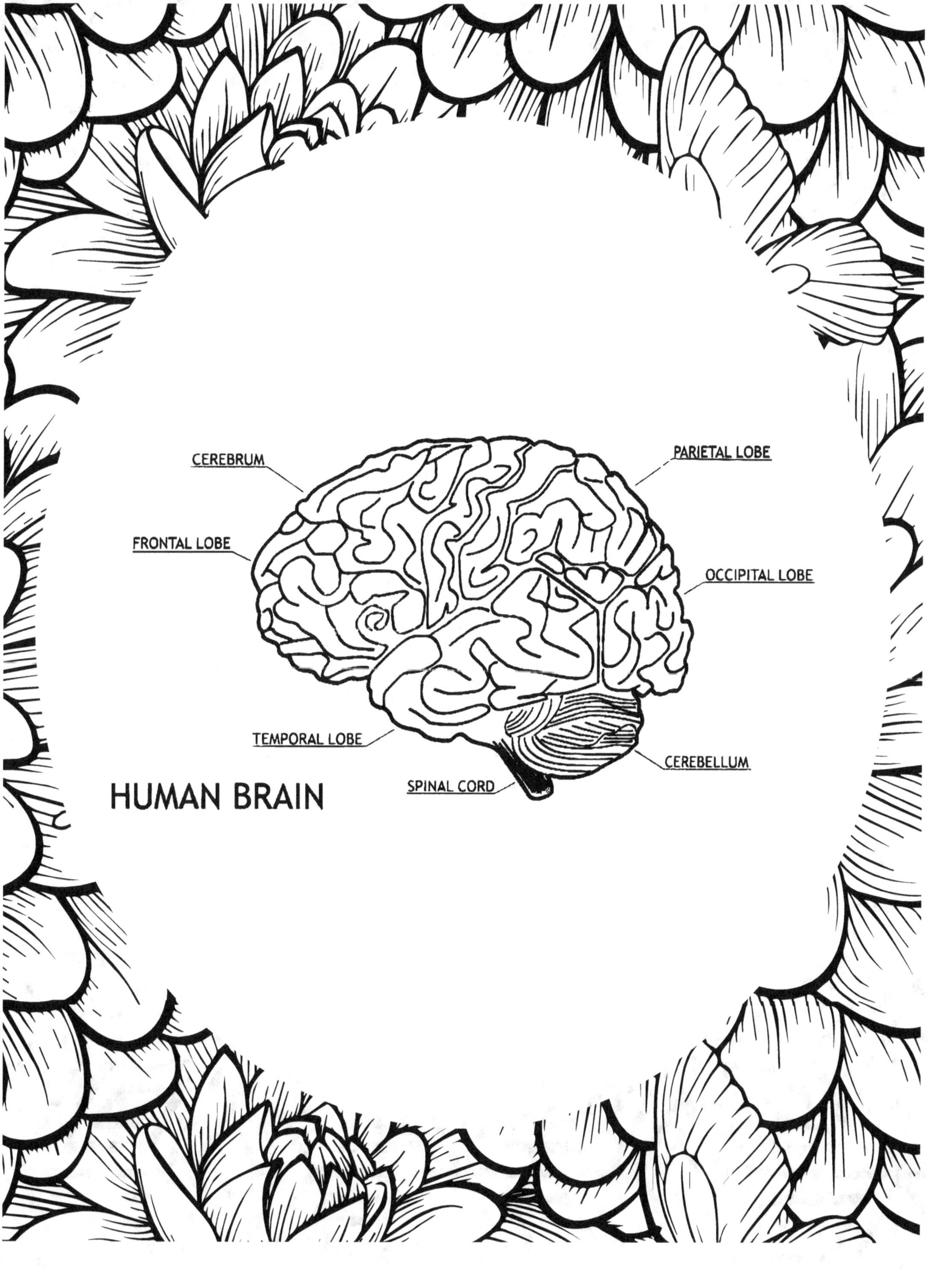
CEREBRUM
PARIETAL LOBE
FRONTAL LOBE
OCCIPITAL LOBE
TEMPORAL LOBE
CEREBELLUM
SPINAL CORD
HUMAN BRAIN

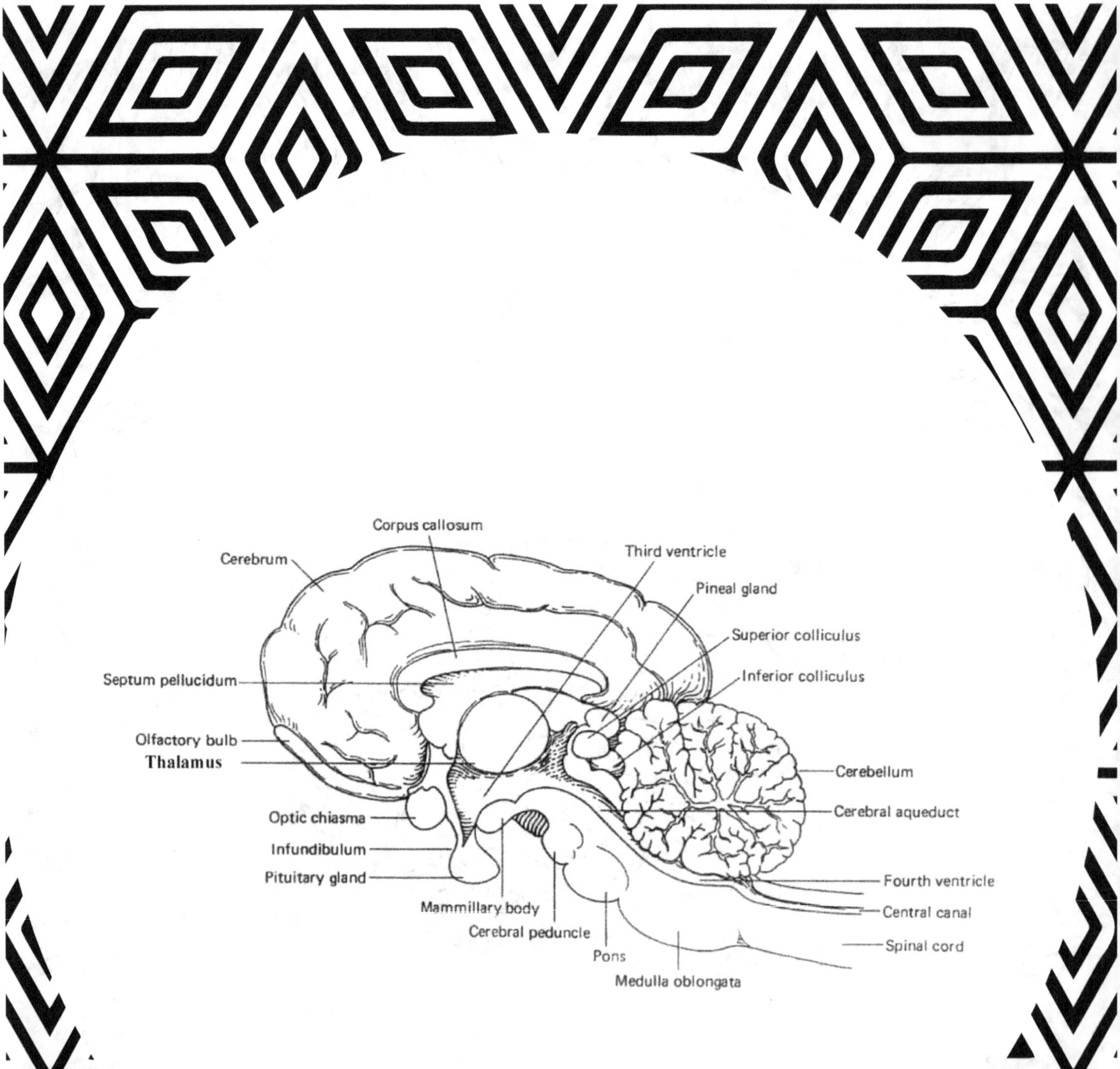
Corpus callosum
Cerebrum
Third ventricle
Pineal gland
Superior colliculus
Septum pellucidum
Inferior colliculus
Olfactory bulb
Thalamus
Cerebellum
Optic chiasma
Cerebral aqueduct
Infundibulum
Pituitary gland
Fourth ventricle
Mammillary body
Central canal
Cerebral peduncle
Spinal cord
Pons
Medulla oblongata

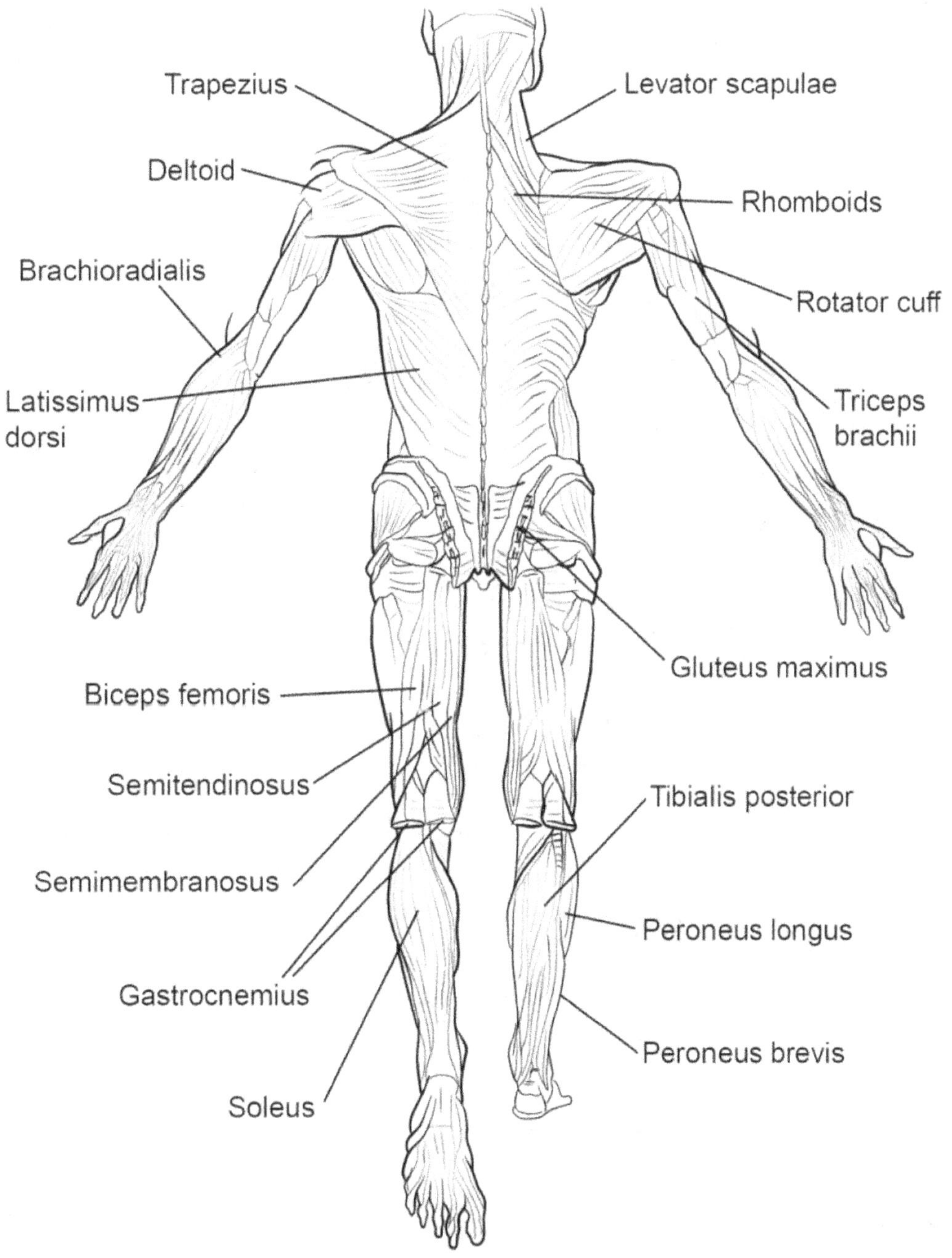

Human Muscles

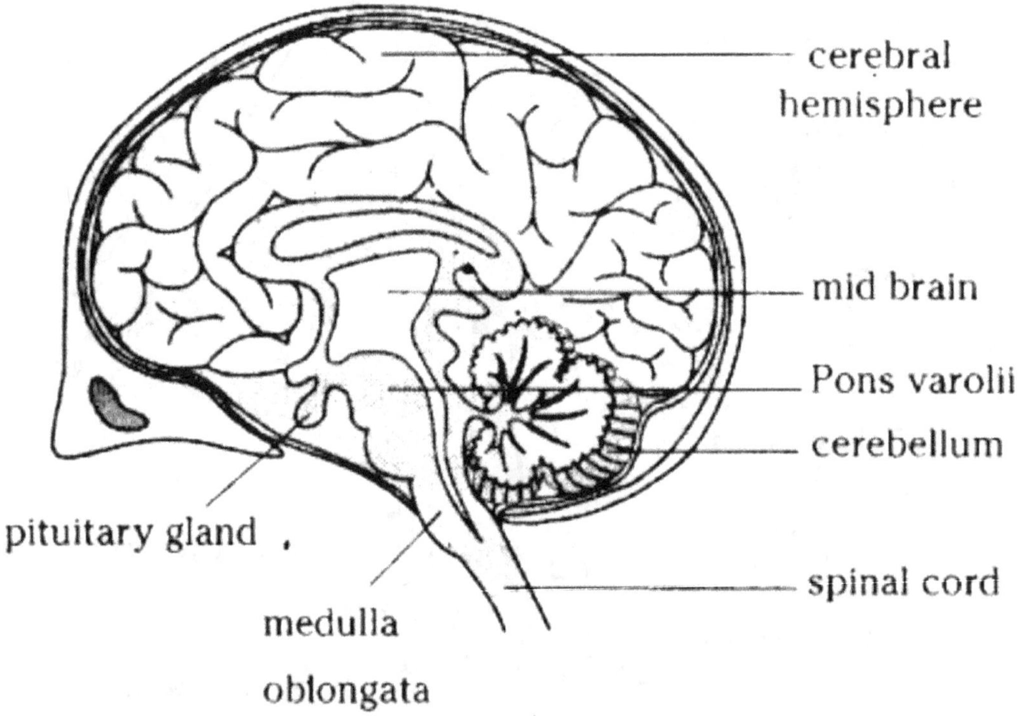
cerebral
hemisphere
mid brain
Pons varolii
cerebellum
pituitary gland
spinal cord
medulla
oblongata

Brain

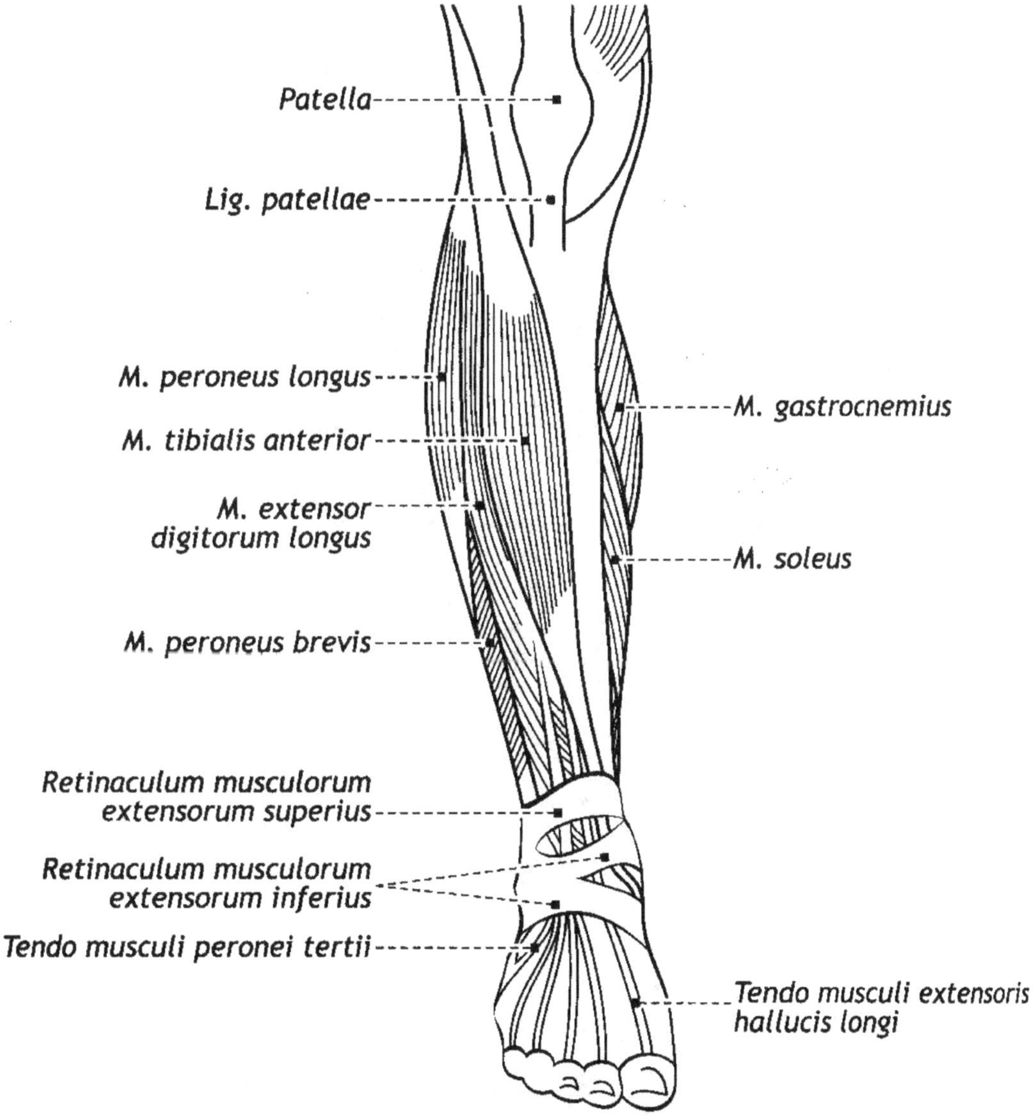

Patella
Lig. patellae
M. peroneus longus
M. tibialis anterior
M. extensor digitorum longus
M. peroneus brevis
Retinaculum musculorum extensorum superius
Retinaculum musculorum extensorum inferius
Tendo musculi peronei tertii
M. gastrocnemius
M. soleus
Tendo musculi extensoris hallucis longi

Color the Bony Features of the Pelvis

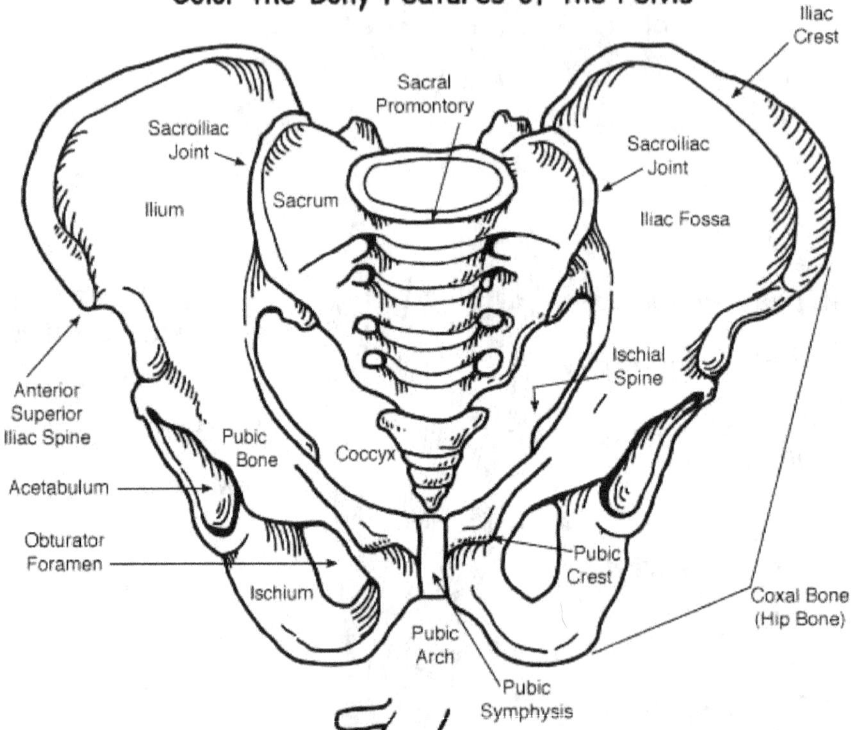

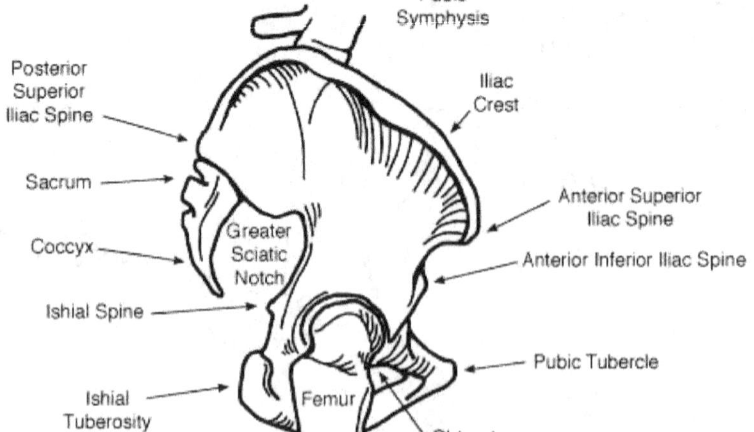

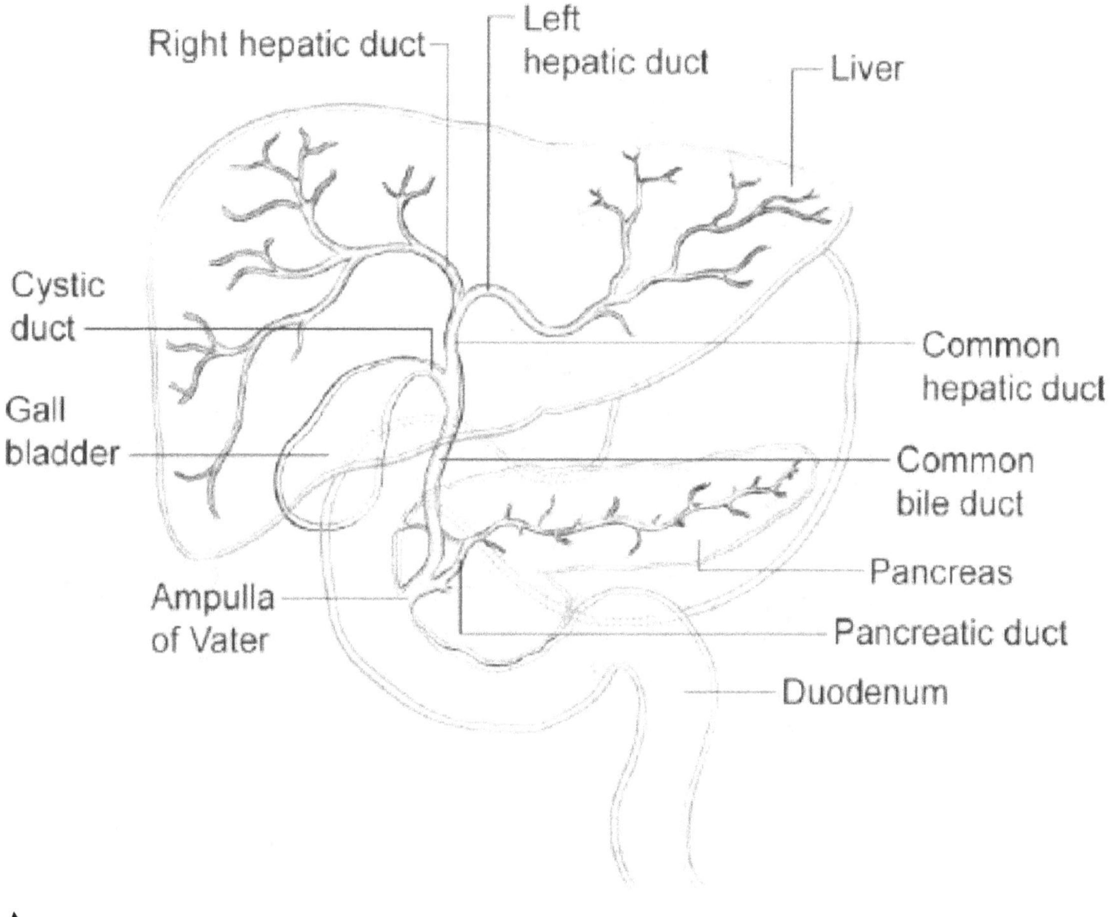
Right hepatic duct
Left hepatic duct
Liver
Cystic duct
Gall bladder
Common hepatic duct
Common bile duct
Pancreas
Ampulla of Vater
Pancreatic duct
Duodenum

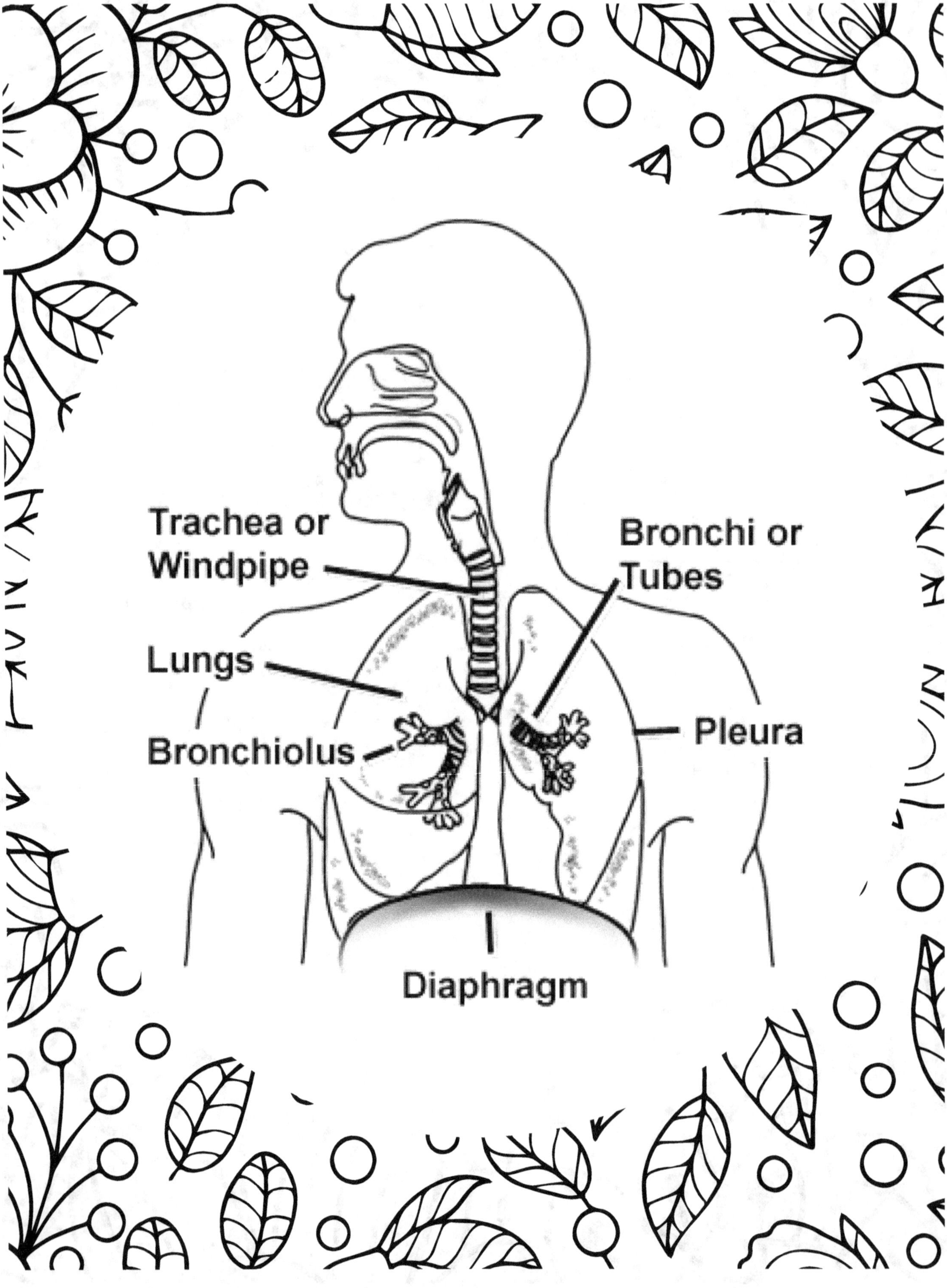
Trachea or
Windpipe
Bronchi or
Tubes
Lungs
Pleura
Bronchiolus
Diaphragm

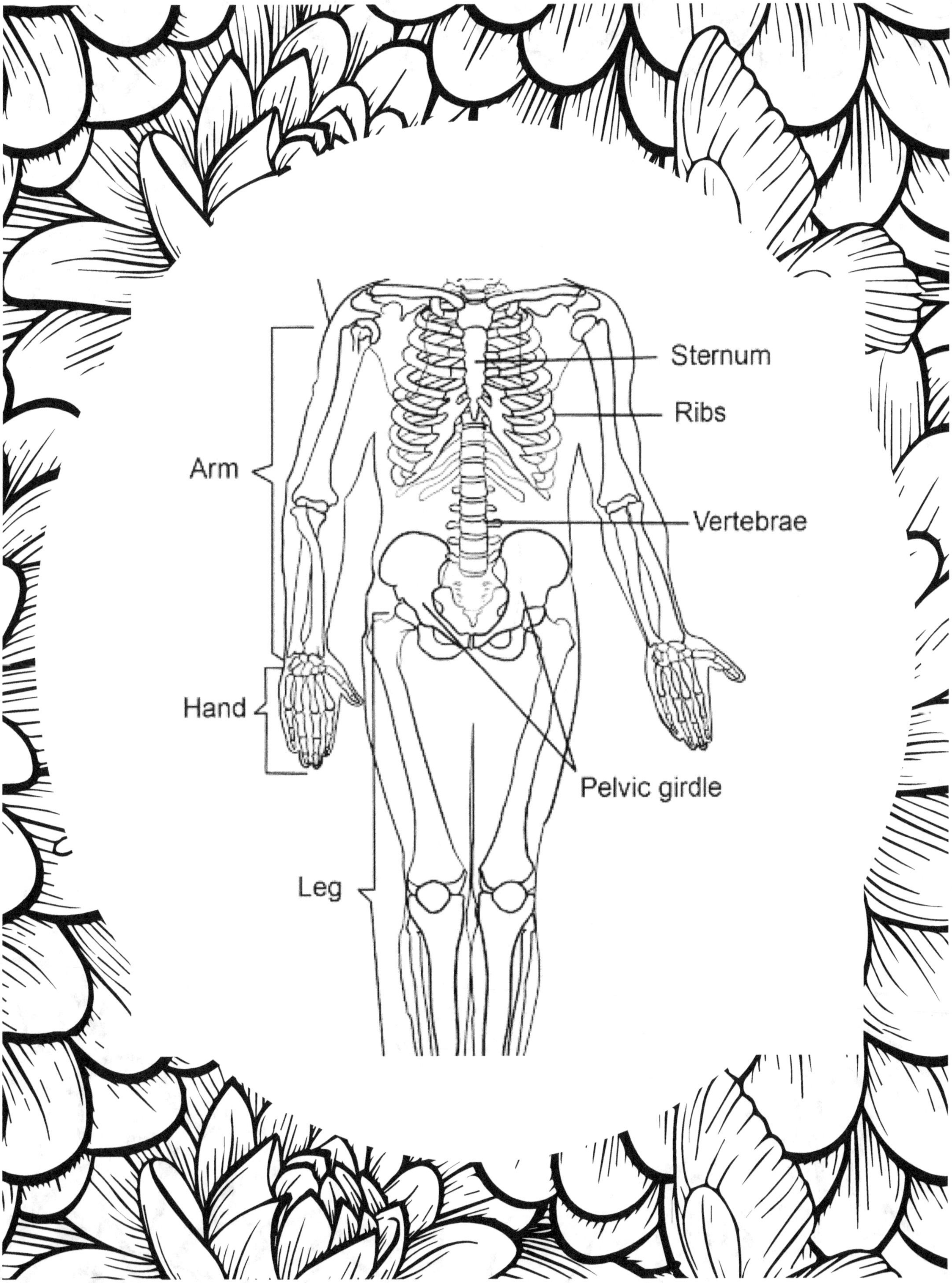
Sternum
Ribs
Arm
Vertebrae
Hand
Pelvic girdle
Leg

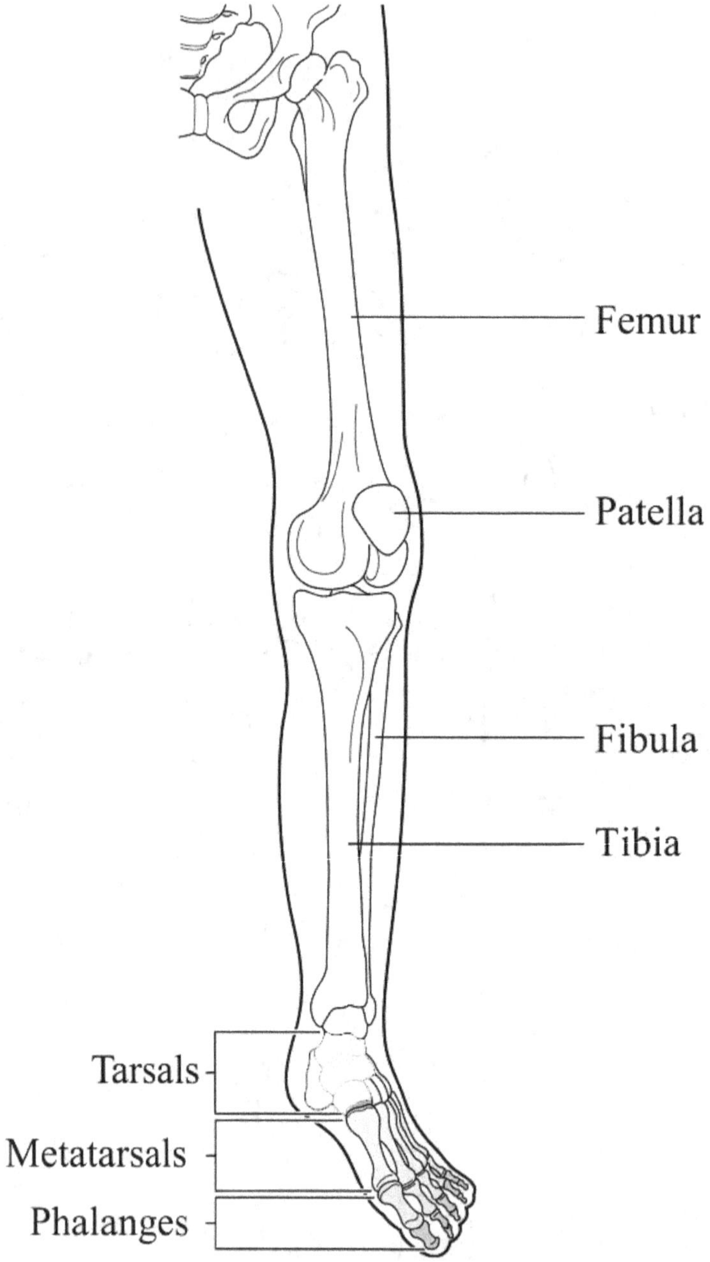
Femur
Patella
Fibula
Tibia
Tarsals
Metatarsals
Phalanges

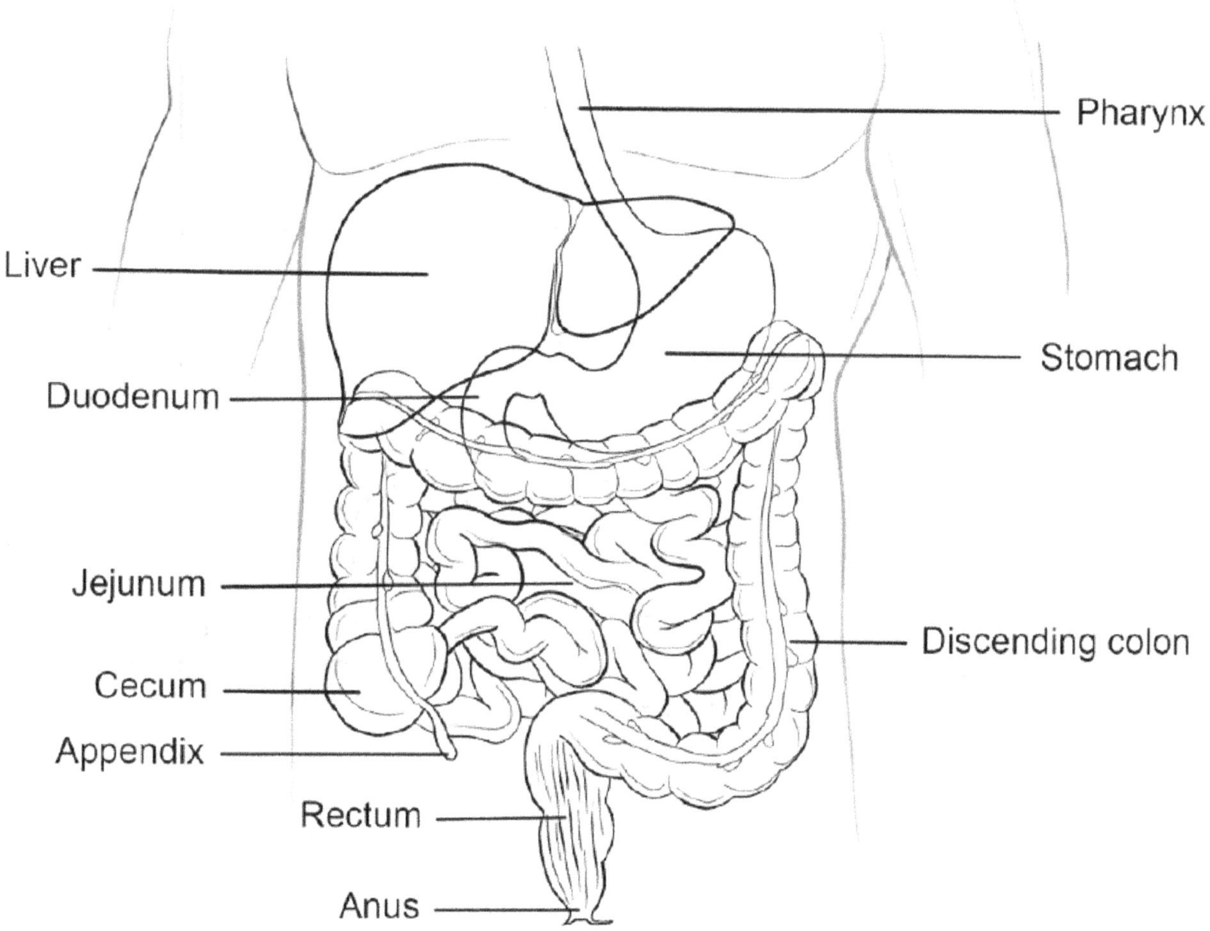
Pharynx
Liver
Stomach
Duodenum
Jejunum
Discending colon
Cecum
Appendix
Rectum
Anus

Kidney Anatomy

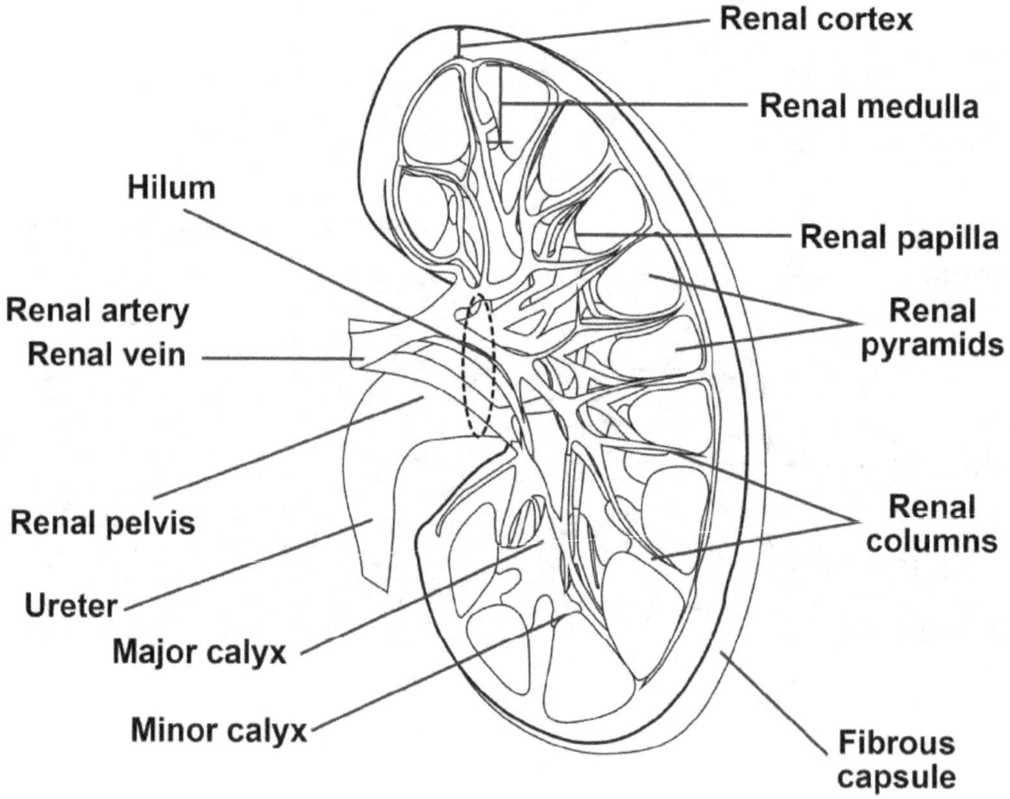

Color the Arteries of the Head and Neck

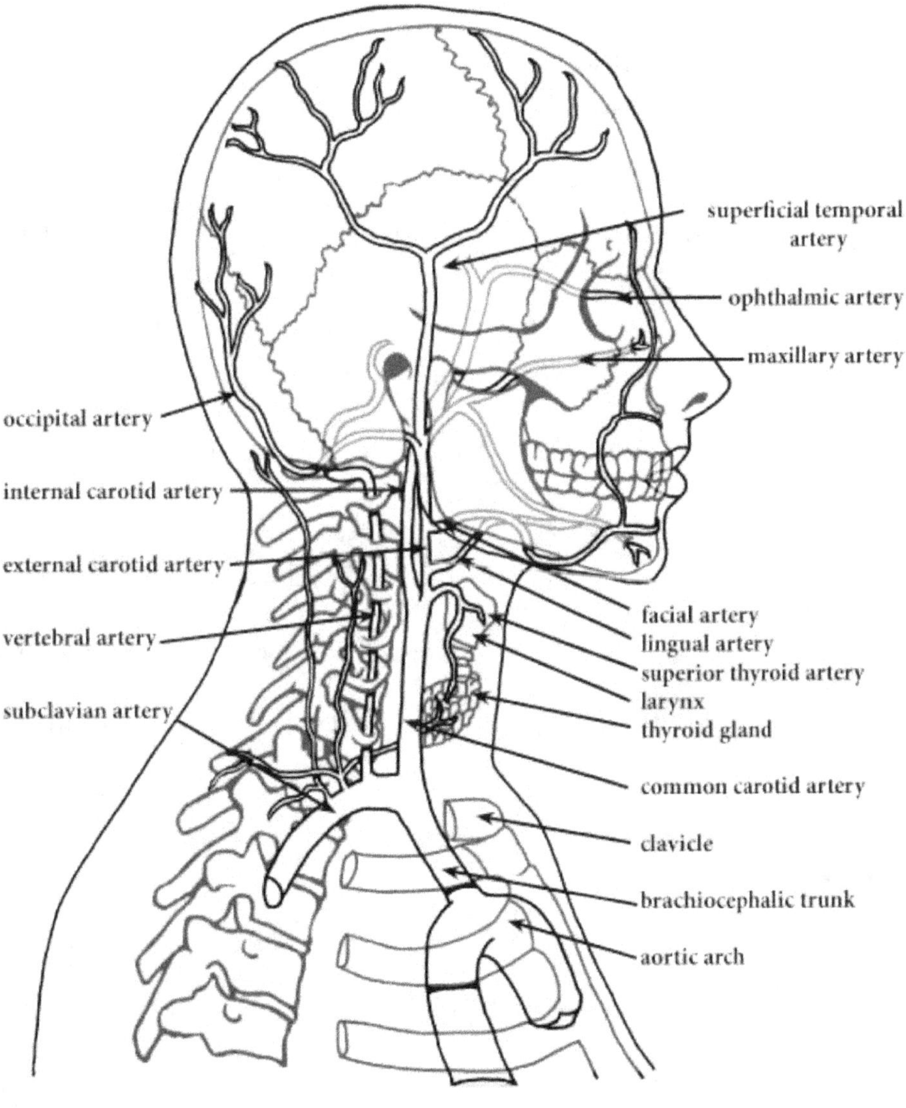

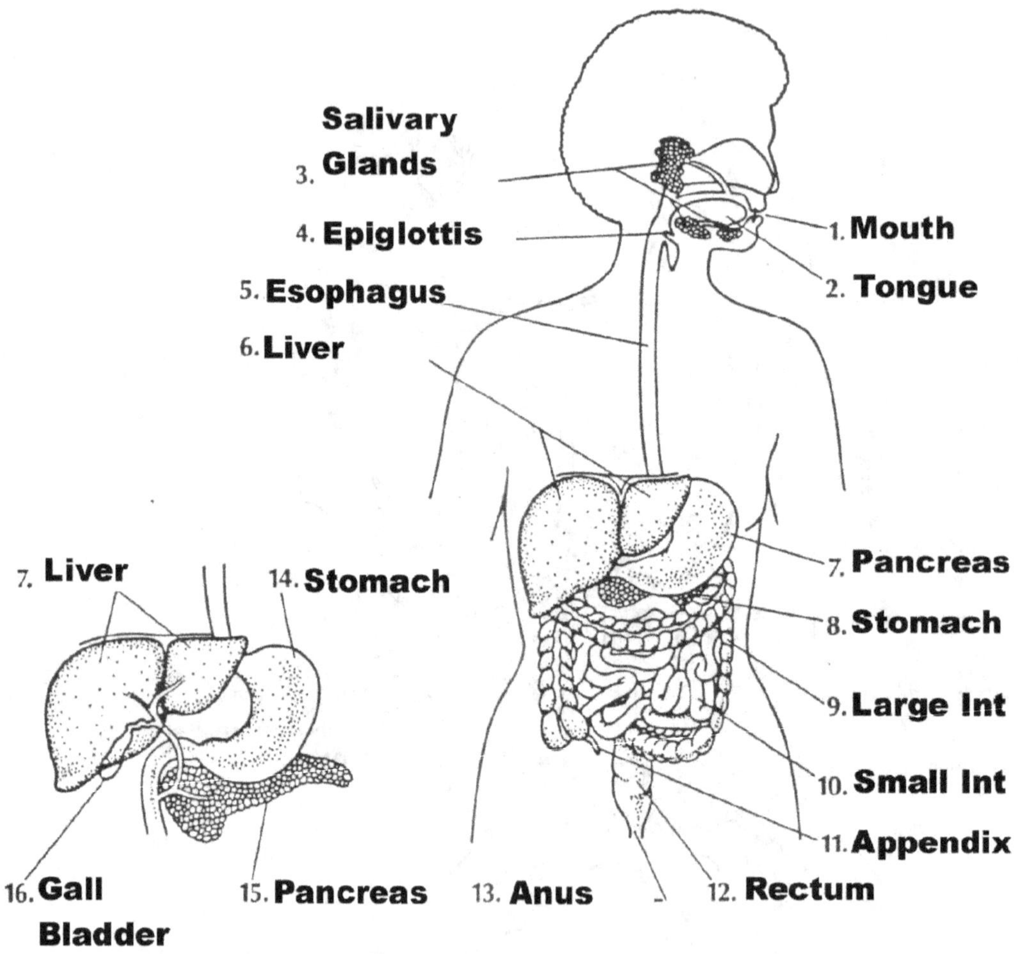
Salivary
3. Glands
4. Epiglottis
5. Esophagus
6. Liver
1. Mouth
2. Tongue
7. Pancreas
8. Stomach
9. Large Int
10. Small Int
11. Appendix
12. Rectum
13. Anus
7. Liver
14. Stomach
15. Pancreas
16. Gall Bladder

www.ingramcontent.com/pod-product-compliance
Lightning Source LLC
Chambersburg PA
CBHW081701220526
45466CB00009B/2841
* 9 7 9 8 5 6 6 1 5 2 6 6 0 *